beauty and the beast

beauty and the beast

MICHAEL TAUSSIG

THE UNIVERSITY OF CHICAGO PRESS

CHICAGO AND LONDON

MICHAEL TAUSSIG is the Class of 1933 Professor of Anthropology
at Columbia University. He is the author of many books, including
I Swear I Saw This, Walter Benjamin's Grave, and *My Cocaine Museum,*
all published by the University of Chicago Press.

The University of Chicago Press, Chicago 60637
The University of Chicago Press, Ltd., London
© 2012 by The University of Chicago
All rights reserved. Published 2012.
Printed in the United States of America

21 20 19 18 17 16 15 14 13 12   1 2 3 4 5

ISBN-13: 978-0-226-78985-9 (cloth)
ISBN-13: 978-0-226-78986-6 (paper)
ISBN-10: 0-226-78985-3 (cloth)
ISBN-10: 0-226-78986-1 (paper)

Library of Congress Cataloging-in-Publication Data

Taussig, Michael T.
    Beauty and the beast / Michael Taussig.
        pages. cm.
    Includes bibliographical references and index.
    ISBN 978-0-226-78985-9 (cloth : alkaline paper)
    ISBN 0-226-78985-3 (cloth : alkaline paper)
    ISBN 978-0-226-78986-6 (paperback : alkaline paper)
    ISBN 0-226-78986-1 (paperback : alkaline paper)
    1. Beauty, Personal. 2. Beauty culture. 3. Surgery, Plastic.
    I. Title.
GT499.T39 2012
646.7—dc23
                                              2011050372

The bartender's smile widened. His ugliness was the stuff of legend. In an age of affordable beauty, there was something heraldic about his lack of it.

WILLIAM GIBSON, *Neuromancer*

contents

author's note

Beauty and the Beast poses the question of beauty in relation to violence, wondering why so many stories in Colombia about cosmetic
surgery—which the author calls "cosmic surgery"—take delight in
the death or disfigurement of the patient. For what is involved is not
simply the coexistence of glamor and terror in the world around us
today, but their synergism.

If, therefore, I choose to write about this in a fairytale mode, it is
to heighten, not diminish, reality, as well as its aesthetic surge, for
is there not a powerful aesthetic at the heart of terror? Is there not
glamor galore in being a throat-cutting paramilitary, a badass narco,
or a street gang member, flouting all the rules and them some? The
mix of charisma and loathing attached to the more spectacularly well
known paramilitaries and narcos is of a piece with their stables of
beautiful women, beautiful horses, and majestic fleets of black SUVs.
Gang members in the slums are not quite so elevated, of course, but
they have their motorbikes and dreams, and are no less beholden to
startling techniques of bodily dismemberment, although they are
likely to be even more inventive with language, haircuts, clothing,
and percussion grenades than the really bad guys at the top.

How much here is true and how much fantasy is a fair enough
question, so long as it assumes their insufferable fusion, which is
another reason to be aware of what we all knew but didn't know
we knew—that aesthetics is as crucial to the tough guys and the
state as it is to bigger breasts, face lifts, or willowy thinness through
liposuction. Surely the endless images and sounds of police with
masks, bulletproof vests, machine guns, shiny black riot gear, heli-

copters, flashing lights, wailing sirens, teargas, and horses—surely these evince as much an aesthetic choice as something we might call "practical" or "utilitarian"? Indeed, is there *anything* "practical" that does not embody an aesthetic?

To my mind this revolves around the *narcolook*, modeled on young women who belong, or wish to belong, to the fabulously wealthy drug traffickers and their over-the-top lifestyles. Their *imago*—silicone breasts, expanded ass, liposuction thinness—has given rise to a boom in fashion and beautification that not only absorbs male as well as female energies and fantasy, but speaks more generally to the body as emblem and vehicle for a way of being that has displaced work and discipline in favor of style, transgression, and eroticized excess. This same aesthetic now sweeps the world to encompass war, torture, mutilation, and the frenzy of the new capitalist economy seeking respite in what is called, all too sedately, "consumption." Colombia is not alone. Nor unique. Just more obvious.

So much for the bad guys, the good guys, and the beautiful women, horses, and SUVs. So much for the underground and the forces of state repression. How could we possibly think of this wondrous mix—for mix it surely is—as one in which aesthetics is not as crucial as the magic aura it creates? But what then of my stories—stories of catastrophe following on cosmic surgery?

"Beauty is always doomed," writes William Burroughs in *Ghost of Chance*. Is that why it shimmers so?

gift of the gods

IS BEAUTY DESTINED TO END IN TRAGEDY?

What a question! Does it not incur the worst of superstition, a dimly sensed unease that too much of something wonderful leads to too much of something terrible? Does it not suggest that beauty is at root inseparable from terror? Meanwhile, most everything else in the world around us, at least until yesterday, was saying you can have it all, the more the merrier. So what gives with this flash of recognition that beauty lives cheek by jowl with tragedy, or that now as I write, in 2009, we are being told that capitalism is tanking because of years of living high on the hog? Even the economists, masters of rational analysis, know deep down that the economy is but a gloss on fairy-tale logic. Take this recent statement by a Nobel Prize winner in economics: "If you want to know where the global crisis comes from, then think of it this way: we're looking at the revenge of the glut."[1]

Could it be that beauty is a gift of the gods that, like all gifts, comes with a measure of anxiety, only in this case, being a gift of the gods, the burden is close to overwhelming? And is this not just as likely to hold for the fairy-tale realities woven around that euphemism known as progress—more accurately, "the domination of nature"—which now very much includes the surgical intervention on the female body we call cosmetic surgery but which, after due consideration, I now call *cosmic* surgery? In Latin America this is but the latest expression of the colonial baroque, with its "exaggerated aestheticism," artificiality, *and* transgression. What else can you

1

call the current irruption of surgeries to produce bigger and better breasts and asses and calves, not to mention surgeries on the eyelids and labia, vaginal rejuvenation, face-lifting, and, of course, becoming thin with liposuction? And that is just the start. There are so many more interventions, inventions, and return visits, like the monthly Botox and "touch up," the *retoque*.

Surely it is the case that cosmic surgery was among the first technologies in the great drama of the domination of nature, and that beauty has been as much a goal in life as the quest for food and shelter. Surely the aesthetic saturates the arts of survival in the societies studied by anthropologists well into the twentieth century. If hunting and gathering technologies, making bows and blowpipes and canoes, along with techniques of voyaging across vast deserts and oceans, spinning fibers, weaving cloth, building houses, and the great galaxy of the arts of kinship and ritual are bountifully present, so is being gorgeous and handsome and fastidious about one's appearance. In what the celebrated Marcel Mauss called archaic societies, the economy (based on the gift) is at once religious, magical, political—and aesthetic.

Take heed of the dazzling body painting, fantastic hairdressing, incisions of one sort or another, genital and elsewhere, filing or removal of teeth, amputation of fingers, stretching of earlobes, labia, and necks to unbelievable lengths, flattening of heads of newborn babes, fattening of calf muscles, pharmacopoeias of potions required for beauty magic and love magic (see Malinowski's *Sexual Life of Savages* for starters), and so forth, on and on, very much including surgical intervention. And in all these triumphs of the "domination of nature" it would be most difficult to separate religion or magic from aesthetics, as both join the emotional power and bodily excitement of the beautiful as force.

What sort of force? To read Evans-Pritchard's account of the love of cattle by the Nuer of Africa in the 1930s is to be struck by the role of beauty and cosmic surgery as sacred force in this relationship of man with beast. A young man takes his personal name from the ox his father has given him at initiation, at which time his forehead is incised with markings and the horn of the ox is cut at an angle so it will eventually cross the muzzle or veer upward. If he can procure metal, the young man will at that same time bind his left arm in such a way as to render it useless, just as the left horn of the ox is rendered useless—making the ox more beautiful and therefore all the more perfect for sacrifice.

For underlying this identification of man with ox is the sacrifice of oxen, it being Evans-Pritchard's opinion that the fundamental idea behind the ritualized killing of this beautiful and beautified animal, which is frequent among the Nuer, is the giving to God of the gift of life, what the philosopher, pornographer, aesthetician, and surrealist Georges Bataille conceptualized as *depense*, or *toomuchness*.[2] Indeed, to read accounts of sacrifice is to be struck by the connection between beauty and life, meaning the taking of life, as with the beautification, hence deification, of the human victim for several months prior to his murder in Aztec sacrifice and of the Vedic Hindu preparation of the person for whom the sacrifice of an animal is being made.[3]

Anthropologists have spent a great deal of energy describing symbols active in social life, and this is well and good. But have we not because of this very focus missed the larger and more important influence of beauty in shaping and energizing society and history, beauty not as form but as force? And likewise, have we not ignored not only the aesthetic shaping of everyday life but the aesthetic shaping of terror as well? Is not the synergism between beauty and what I will call the "negative sublime" as much the motor of history as are the means of production of material life?

It was all there, actually, from the beginning, in Malinowski's patient attention to the islanders' untiring attention to the aesthetics of every phase of their farming—the clearing, the planting of tubers, the weeding, the tending of the sculptural quality of climbing vines, the magic associated with each stage, and, of course, the exquisite care for the display of those ungainly tubers at harvest, left in the center of the village till they rot. It was all so beautiful, beginning with the title, *Coral Gardens and Their Magic* (two whole volumes). It was all so aesthetic, not only the dances with the oiling and perfuming of the body and the sculpture of the gardens, but the *kula* ornaments too, the red shell necklaces and the white shell bracelets, around which interisland trade revolved and depended, not to mention storytelling of fantastic voyages and dreams of untold excess:

> My fame is like thunder
> My steps are like earthquake[4]

It was all there, actually, from the beginning, in Malinowski's description of women witches who make themselves invisible, flying though the night to feed off the eyes, tongue, and intestines of a fresh corpse, striking terror in the hearts of men. They turn beauty inside out; that is the way of the witch, that is how you can tell a witch. As young girls, potential witches can be detected by their crude tastes. When a pig is quartered they will drink its blood and tear at its flesh.

Shipwrecked sailors dread witches and therefore recite spells over a root of ginger, spells uttered in a rhythmic and alliterative manner, so as to create a mist that will befog the witch. Maybe it is to befog themselves as well and prevent them seeing the witch's loathsome being:

> The mist springs up
> The mist makes them tremble

Like Evans-Pritchard describing the beliefs in witches among the Zande of Central Africa, Malinowski hastens to assure us that the native "feels and fears his belief rather than formulates it clearly to himself."[5] Feels and fears. In other words, not so much words and not so much "belief" as feelings and fears that arise from images and potent shapes. Is that something emotional or aesthetic, or both? Surely the fear at issue here, the fear of aerial witches roaming the night skies like fireflies, is emotional *and* aesthetic, and it would be wrongheaded to translate such affective and aesthetic intensities into a principle of belief. The idea of the witch is at once an emotion and a picture cast in cascading images of repulsion. It is the possibility, the haze on the horizon of possibilities associated with death and the corpse. To talk here of belief, let alone principles of belief, is to forsake what is potent so as to claim the safe ground of a verbal terra firma hostile to the dangerous realm of images and feeling. Plato's *Republic* is built on this terra firma.

The belief in evil here is patently aesthetic, a chilling sense of the ugliness of the unappeasable appetite for all that is morally wrong—indeed incomprehensible, a veritable charter of the loathsome and the tabooed. How fitting that another aesthetic force should be mobilized against these awful creatures, and those corpses and eyes and tongues, namely the aesthetic of the spell as poetry, which extends for two pages of closely written text, with wondrous metaphors, rhythm, and alliteration, ending with the poet-magician covering the naked body of the imagined witch:

> I take thy sleeping grass skirt
> I cover thy loins
> Remain there; snore within[6]

Be it noted that to the extent that beauty magic is equivalent to love magic (as described by Malinowski), such beauty is likely to be aimed at feeling the charge, making the charge:

> My head, it flares up
> It flashes,
> My red paint, it flares up
> It flashes[7]

Which I assume is more than enough. Who wants more than to put charge into the world, beginning with oneself? But beauty is more than a thing-in-itself. It speaks to someone or something. There is that other person or god to be attracted, to be attractive to, to be seduced—not just for sexual love but as trading partners, man to man, as in the charged exchange of kula valuables. But then who said trade was sexless, especially when it is conducted under the magical auspices associated with gifting the gift?

Could it be, then, that aesthetics are what prime the pump of life? Only in our modern haste to reduce everything to a means to an end, an efficient means to an ever-receding end, we are confused, and mightily so, by the place of art. Having elevated art as both commodity and metaphysical substance, having imprisoned art in museums, galleries, and boardrooms, having thus separated art from the artisan, having opposed "art" to the "useful," have we not become blind to the force of the aesthetic, of beauty, if you will, coursing through everyday life? Surely beauty is as as much infrastructure as are highways and bridges, storytelling and the Internet, rainfall and global warming?

But I sense something wrong in this way of looking at things. Simply inverting what was superstructure, namely the aesthetic, and calling it infrastructure is not good enough. What is lacking has to do with what Mauss in his book on the gift called "the total social fact," in which magic and the aesthetic are inseparable from the economic. He had in mind the economy of the Trobriands and the American Northwest, famous for the potlatch. But what I have in mind is the contemporary globalized economy. Not only is the inseparability of the aesthetic and the magic of the economy now *back* in the saddle but, under the rubric of the postmodern, new worlds of aesthetic intensification and libidinal gratification bound to a new body have taken center stage.

Not only gardens but the gods too are to be won over by beauty— and all this aesthetic lore and artisanry beautifying the work of man can be seen more generally as what goes into designing the world, giving it its "makeover" as well as its *retoque*, or "touch-up," as we say today with regard to cosmic surgery.We may call this culture, and the point then seems obvious that cultures have an aesthetic or several thereof perhaps in stark conflict. More to the point is the dependence on the aesthetic. Something as basic as a language, for instance, not only has its aesthetic but is dependent on such. The flow of sound, the rhythms and cadence, let alone the play and inventiveness, respond to aesthetic desires and aesthetic principles as much as semiotic considerations. And as for language so for all of culture, which can be viewed as *design*, continuously entertained and indulged. Cosmic surgery provides a stark example of this poesis, which to my mind is present as an active force in designing a new body, a new face, a smile for a paramilitary mass murderer, an airplane, a spark plug, a computer chip, in giving a name to a person, or in a Ronald Reagan ("the Great Communicator") using communication to win elections.

How strange, then, that in this our modern culture we feel it right and natural that design, as such, that beauty, as such, from gods to gardens, should be understood not as infrastructure but as mere ornament—and too much ornament as distasteful. For if my examples so far indicate that bodily beautification entails cosmic concerns, implicating therefore magic and ritual as well as a sense of myth, poetry, and the marvelous, I have to ask, what is bodily beauty today, now that the connection between the body and the stars has long since been cut?

Yet despite—or because of—this free fall, are we not experiencing a sudden rise, nay, a revolution, in surgeries meant to make us look good or better? Do not these procedures, like damming rivers and moon shots, no less than trading in bicycles for automobiles, test, in the language implicit to fairy tales, the patience of the gods? For unlike fairy tales with happy endings, in which Jack defeats the giant and Beauty's tears restore the Beast to his handsome princely self, the tales I have in mind from the agribusiness slums of Colombia are emissions from the dark side of beauty, tales of misfortune that find grim satisfaction in attempts at beautification gone tragically wrong: the breast enlargement that ends with infection and double mastectomy; eye surgery that instead of making you a wide-eyed beauty ends with you not being able to close your eyes day or night; the facelift that twists your most prized possession into horror-movie grotesquerie, neck tendons standing out like the guylines supporting a circus tent; ass uplift or enlargement that slowly slides down the back of your legs—or kills you, as happened to the abolutely gorgeous Solange Magnano, thirty-seven years old and a former Miss Argentina, in 2009; or liposuction that not only sucks out your fat but kills you on the operating table on account of the anesthetic or a day or two later because of desanguination. So the gods return, the connection with the stars returns—this time as disaster.

I imagine most fairy tales were like this, horror stories mixed with potent fantasies about the body and heedless ambition, before they were sanitized by Disney as bedside pabulum for children and their parents. "And they all lived happily ever after." The hope that lives in the fairy tale is there in every story, says Walter Benjamin, who is of the opinion that the fairy tale lives on secretly in every story—and yet he insists it is death that grants the storyteller authority.[8] Death and hope are reconciled—if that's the word—because what death does is refer the story to *natural history no less than to the supernatural.* And what could be more natural, may I ask, more historical, or more supernatural—all at once—than the human face and human body reconfigured by cosmic surgery?

Let us for the moment think of the face and the body as a jewel and recall Bataille's argument that a jewel—magical and glowing with an inner fire—lends itself to what he called *depense.* This is usually translated as "expenditure," or "profitless expenditure," but that does not seem to me nearly strong enough for what Bataille wants to get at, which is the big flame-out, the passion within the gift, going for broke, living in the fast lane, burning your bridges, etc. *Excess* is another word that looms large here: excessive wanting, excessive spending, excessive consuming and the devil take the hindmost. High on a mix of hashish and a morphine derivative in 1931, Benjamin put it rather well: "To cast purpose to the winds is a properly sporting activity."[9] As for Bataille: "The sun gives without receiving."

"I had a point of view," Bataille wrote in the late 1940s, settling ever so seriously into what he considered his major work, *The Accursed Share*. "I had a point of view from which a human sacrifice, the construction of a church or the gift of a jewel were no less interesting than the sale of wheat. In short I had to try in vain to make clear the notion of a 'general economy' in which the 'expenditure' (the 'consumption') of wealth, rather than production, was the primary object."[10]

To that list, of course, we must add cosmic surgery and the arts of terror. Each, let alone the two combined, would seem to be at the very center of Bataille's general economy.

Let us recall Benjamin recounting the story by the nineteenth-century Russian Nikolai Leskov concerning a precious stone from Siberia, a chrysoberyl called the Alexandrite. It is the deep-in-the-earth home of such stones that assures them prodigous spiritual powers, especially when shaped by the jewel cutter (read, surgeon), who in Leskov's story is obviously a magician as well as a skilled craftsman. Such, in my reckoning, is the human face and the human body readying itself for cosmic surgery: a face and a body prodigously ripe with spiritual power, like the jewel, both natural and supernatural, awaiting the deft touch of the jewel cutter.

But why should people who comment on cosmic surgery choose to concentrate on the failures (which presumably are less frequent than the successes)? It seems that cosmic surgery taps into a deep vein of discomfort. Death or disfiguration due to cosmic surgery is not fair. That's for sure. But that's not what my stories are about. Think of their shape. Think of their rearing and plunging, reaching out for beauty as of eye, breast, face, and willowy thinness, and then waking up shatteringly ugly, or worse, if there be a worse. These stories are about the sudden dive into the abyss at a moment when the very heavens were in your reach. They are like the old stories about selling your soul to the devil or what tough guys playing the realism card mean when they say, "There's no such thing as a free lunch." Sometimes they add, "my friend."

The first tale of misfortune I have in mind is the swerve by doctors from treating bodily illness to treating bodily appearance. The number one choice of specialization for medical graduates in the United States today is dermatology—or should I say "dermatology"?—very much including cosmic surgery. "It is an unfortunate circumstance that you can spend an hour with a patient treating them for diabetes and hypertension and make $100, or you can do Botox and make $2,000 in the same time," says Eric Parlette, a dermatologist in Massachussets, as reported in the *New York Times*.[11] Small wonder there is a shortage in the USA of primary care or family doctors. You don't have to be superstitious to feel uncomfortable at this turn of events sweeping the world. If you think it is restricted to Miami or LA, check out Beirut, Cali, or Medellin, notorious for their mix of poverty, violence, liposuction, breast enlargement, face-lifting, ass enlargement, and restoration of the hymen. I can hear a famous queen who is reported to have said, "Bread? Let them eat cake!" now saying, "Cake? Let them have a face-lift!"

This much-criticized queen was ahead of her time. She understood what is important in life, and in this she predates by two centuries our philosopher of consumption, Georges Bataille, with his belief that the principle of utility was insufficient for understanding human societies or people. To the contrary, the exuberance of *depense* or unproductive spending (cake versus bread) drove all economic systems, even the production-oriented capitalism of his time, so distinct from today's economy of delirious consumption.

Take Bataille's approach to the beauty of flowers, which he regards as intimately tied to death and decay. What grants flowers their beauty, in his opinion, has a lot to do with their short life span, meaning the ugliness that is their fate, the withering on the stem, petals tired, drooping, discolored, dropping one by one to dissolve in the manure of the flower bed or be swept away as garbage. Leaves may age honestly, but it is flowers, not leaves, that we present at dinner parties, birthdays, weddings, and funerals.[12]

Bataille does not go this far but I would ask, if it is the proximity of decay and death that makes beauty beautiful, then can we not see this as part of the cycle of endless return of a millennial rhythm and millennial hope—the rhythm, long preceeding Christianity, of resurrection following decay and death, as with spring flowers succeeding winter?

In *The Golden Bough* Frazer tells us how a great mother goddess personifying the reproductive energies of nature was worshipped by many peoples of the Middle East. The caption to a color illustration of a flower, a scarlet anemone, in an illustrated version of Frazer's great book, tells us how "spring flowers spoke to the ancients of the resurrection of their gods, while the fading of the same flowers reminded them of their death."[13]

Cosmic surgery contests this eternal rhythm by trying to hold the female body in a continuous springtime, yet the connection and tension between death and beauty remains. Could it be that the beauty of women today echoes those remote times when people worshipped a female deity whose power was expressed in the passing of the seasons? This is why fashion in women's clothes has its annual rhythm, yet another instance of the power of sympathetic magic.

Not only that, but with the ascension of patriarchy and the displacement of Frazer's great mother goddess, Christ himself came to embody that older fascination, previously restricted to woman, with seasonal death and resurrection. Christ is that cyclically restored woman. And now, is not cosmic surgery itself a replay of spring following winter, not to mention a replay of the redemption achieved through crucifixion? Small wonder that the body thus redeemed exudes the ambiguity of sacred power with its fear and awe, its attraction and its repulsion.

So what happened to those goddesses once the male god gained favor? Here's what happened: the death and resurrection of the goddess became secularized as the realm of feminine beauty. Think twice before you mock Colombia's fascination with beauty queens and their attendant cosmic surgeries.

In truth, the alternation of bodily beauty and death manifests itself in a rhythm infinitely more rapid than that of the seasons. In the heart-wrenching stories that concern cosmic surgery gone wrong, stories that anticipate and reflect the mutilations and massacres strewn across rural Colombia for many a decade, this alternation of springtime and winter quivers continuously, 24/7, like a leaf in the storm. For such stories are not just stories of *depense*. They are stories as *depense*. Thus does the death that inspires the art of the storyteller expend itself.

el mexicano

AFTER THE STORY OF THE CAKE QUEEN, the best story of *depense* comes from Colombia. It is said that the notorious cocaine trafficker known as El Mexicano had his toilet paper embossed with his initials in gold—real gold! That's a lot of gold down the chute when you consider how many initials he had. JGRG. José Gonzalo Rodríguez Gacha. And this was long before Mexico became the privileged route for Colombian cocaine. The story no less than the name is prophetic.

Why do people love to tell this story? (It was told me by a rich man in Bogotá, fearful of being kidnapped). El Mexicano was a cruel and powerful man, rich beyond our imagination, rich like kings in ancient fables, a god among men. It is therefore comforting to know that he too has to sit and strain at stool, that he too is subject to bodily evacuation, like any animal, and is thus a mere mortal like the rest of us. Well, not exactly. Not exactly like the rest of us, because he has come down, come down from the heights, from the superhuman to the infrahuman, to the unmentionable parts of our bodies and daily habits. Abjection on this scale, from prince to poo, generates considerable power, like a waterfall. That is why we love this story. One reason anyway. We love the fall of the waterfall. Another reason is its indelible imagery, bringing together gold and poo in a wondrous convergence of opposites that, curiously, seem destined for each other.

This is an old story, the story of money as the root of all evil, the story of gold as cursed—as in B. Traven's Mexican novel *The Treasure of the Sierra Madre*, made into a film by John Huston starring Humphrey Bogart. And it persists even now, when the gold-filled seams of the Sierra Madre have long been replaced by virtual money deals on Wall Street and by throat-cutting cartels peddling cocaine, two sides of the one golden coin.

But there is more to it than this. For the excremental vision of the Mexicano is one that undoes the work of *sublimation*, which uses repression to channel our sensual energy into lofty achievements. Like alchemy, sublimation converts base matter into gold. But in the story of El Mexicano, the reverse occurs; gold reverts to poo, and the alchemists' dream is run backward. Spirit becomes flesh. "I can't tell you," writes the young Freud in December 1897 to his intellectual soul mate in Berlin, Wilhelm Fliess, "how many things I (a new Midas) turn into—filth. This is in complete harmony with the theory of internal stinking. Above all, gold itself stinks."[1] As this process of desublimation strains and heaves, we encounter flesh galore, splattered fragments of human bodies in the form of assassination, mutilation, muscled horseflesh, and body parts of beautiful women subjected to multiple cosmic surgeries.

Is this why we love to tell the story of El Mexicano? For desublimation is anything but straightforward and certainly does not mean a loss of aura. In falling from the heights, the prince may actually be enobled. Sacrilege enhances the god with new powers that emanate from breaking taboos, as when we envisage him straining at stool, reaching for his golden tissue. In this situation extremes meet and then explode, dialectics spin, and like a bolt of lightning, Bataille's *depense* irradiates base matter.

Now the man is dead, shot like a mad dog, surrounded by more than a thousand marines unwittingly led by his silly son Fredy to his father's ranch on the Caribbean coast at Tolú, a village notorious for its female witches according to the Spanish Inquisition of the seventeenth century.

Why do people love to tell this story? Is it because it ends badly, if not sadly, with the JGRG Mexicano become the dead Mexicano, surrounded by more than a thousand marines, by his dead son Fredy, and by the ghosts of all those witches? Why do we like stories that end badly, fairy tales of disaster?

So much for *depense* in stories about drug lords, a notoriously flamboyant lot. What about the *depense* of a guerrilla lord, namely Jacobo Arenas, who for more than three decades shared the leadership of the oldest guerrilla army in the world, the Colombian FARC.

Until his death from natural causes, Arenas lived hidden in the forest-clad mountains of southern Colombia. A young female guerrilla combatant, devoted to him, recalls:

He was extremely vain and loved good things. He would drink only Remy Martin brandy and smoke Kool. Even his shirts and sweaters were tailor-made. When he got you to buy material to make clothes for him, you knew you had to get the most scandalous and garish available. He wore *guyaberas* that nobody else dared wear, with leopard spots—green with purple, gold, and silver. He delighted in the strangest things, such as a machine to count dollars that he saw advertized in a Japanese magazine, corn-cakes sold in Anolaima that were called *"mocosas,"* . . . and he fussed a lot with his huge set of false teeth. He would order a dentist to come to the hideout so he would not be without teeth. Once the dentist noticed that he was coming out in pimples so he advised him to use a cream called *Pomada Peña*. Jacobo ordered two dozen and took an entire box with him when he set out on a trip to the mountain plateaus. He burned his skin and for a month looked like an albino with white spots all over—simply because he was so vain.[2]

In contrast to the *depenses* of El Mexicano, there seems something innocent and childlike to those of Arenas. But the somersault of desublimation and "return" to the body is the same, and it is gold (that is, money) that is crucial to this return. The seemingly infinite amounts of money that the machine in the Japanese magazine can count is combined here not with anal strivings but with the mouth and hence with the breast. The teeth are not only huge like those of an ogre—a nice *depense* touch—but artificial, which is still freakier. Yet as with the fairy tale of Beauty and the Beast, even an ogre can be sweet and gentle and, of all things, can suffer from pimples like a shy adolescent, even if over sixty years of age.

Indeed, according to this story, due to his *depense*-like purchase of skin cream, our beloved ogre of the big teeth has developed unsightly blotches all over his body, resembling the camouflage uniforms the guerrilla, like soldiers and little boys the world over, like to wear. This is not the story of a man converting base matter into gold and gold into base matter, as with JGRG, but the story of a founder of the FARC converting *himself* into gold, into a handsome prince, sans pimples, clad in leopard-print shirts with green, purple, gold, and silver spots. Only the Founding Father could be so wild, so wonderfully *depensish*. Next step? Cosmic surgery, along with a glass or two of Remy Martin and a drag on a Kool. But hold on! Way up there on the mountain plateaus something has happened. The prince our savior has turned into an albino with white spots! What's happened to the leopard!

Why do we love these stories of disaster, stories that rear up to heaven only to crash down in a spasmodic twist of fate?

a rare and
delightful bird
in flight

YOU DON'T HAVE TO BE A DRUG KINGPIN like El Mexicano or a leader of the FARC guerrilla in Colombia to indulge in a bit of *depense* now and again. Take my own stories. In Bogotá's domestic airport when I passed through in 2006, there were men's Italian shoes on display for the equivalent of 290 US dollars—this in a society where the so-called minimum wage was then about eight dollars a day. As for my own *depenses*, a man's haircut costs two dollars, at least where I get my hair cut, by Nima in her salon in a grubby agribusiness town south of the city of Cali in the west of Colombia.

Let me tell you about Nima. As she cuts my hair she is wearing a tight pink swimming costume. Her hair is waist-length, lustrous, brown, and mostly false, what is here called *pelo prestado*, "loaned hair," or an *extension*, which, at that length, could cost a great deal, depending on the quality and how much it costs to have it woven into your real hair. She has had, so I am told, plastic surgery on her nose and who knows where else, her knee-length pants are white and skin tight, and as I wait my turn I see she is applying chemical paste to a woman's hair so as to make it straight. You have to be careful, in applying this paste, not to touch the scalp, as it will burn and stop hair growing for several months. But it will straighten African hair without the use of curlers or hot tongs.

Poor as the town is, style is as much a preoccupation as are the drug-crazed gangs and the terrible economy. Beauty is king. And this is why there is an abundance of beauty salons and why most young women, and even small girls aged seven or younger, are wearing extensions of straight or curly black hair down to the middle of the back or to their hips.

In his essay "The Painter of Modern Life," Baudelaire reminds us that "even in those centuries which seem to us the most monstrous and the maddest, the immortal thirst for beauty has always found its satisfaction."[1] That immortal thirst is certainly active in Nima's town today, with its cult of the body and craze for style and fashion, alongside record levels of violence. Yet it is more than beauty with which beauty dazzles us. It is beauty-as-*depense*, a tsunami of extravagant consumption reaching ever more baroque splendor that is beautiful—that tight pink swimming costume, that caustic cream, that waist-length hair, lustrous, brown, and mainly false.

If Marx and Engels, in *The Communist Manifesto* of 1848, emphasized the Dionysian spirit of capitalism, lurching back and forth in ever grander waves of construction and destruction such that *all that is solid melts into air*, Bataille would say that such melting is what the game is all about, including our strenuous efforts to become more beautiful and hence more desired, both by ourselves and by others. But most Marxists are loath to share the insights of Marx and instead direct scathing, puritanical scorn against people who buy designer clothing, jewelry, trophy houses, trophy wives, and cosmic surgery and thus sustain—in the words of one irate analyst—a "world of pseudo-satisfactions that is superficially exciting but hollow at its core."[2]

Talk about missing the point! Superficial. Exciting. Hollow. This is what it's all about! To vituperate like this is to be born on the wrong side of history and live in denial. What is more, even in our current penny-pinching recession/depression mode, beauty and the need to consume—to expend unprofitably—remains vigorous, perhaps not in dollars spent but certainly in the flaunting of *depense*. Take these stories in the online political daily the *Huffington Post*: in late February 2009 it presented a raft of pictures of the ravishing fifty-something film star Sharon Stone appearing at an AIDS benefit wearing a spectacular, see-through, black lace dress, as well as several pictures of media star Beyonce showing a brief glimpse of her right nipple as she bent way back in a dance pose in a stunning low-cut red dress. A week later it was the turn of Pamela Anderson, who accidentally showed some nipple as she walked the catwalk in Paris with one of Britain's top fashion designers. And so it shows.

"Even in Tough Times, It Seems, a Person Needs Mascara," read the headline of a February 2009 story in the *New York Times,* making much of the *lipstick factor,* the belief that women buy more lipstick during a recession. "Women will always spend on things like lipstick and perfume," said a mother who had sold cosmetics during the Great Depression. A twenty-three-year-old literary agent confirmed this resistence to cutting back, even in a downturn. She had bought a Diptyque firewood-scented candle for her boyfriend and a By Terry concealer and lip treatment for herself at Barneys and received a free cosmetics bag containing samples from twenty vendors (with items like "Lady is a Tramp" nail polish and "Rose Gitane" lip gloss) because her tab came to more than $175.[3] Add to that the fact that Hollywood is reported to be doing well despite the current economic collapse, with attendance at movie houses in the US up 16 percent in 2009 despite an increase in the price of tickets.[4]

And well might women be queuing up for lipstick, given the dismal news early in 2009 that men on Wall Street were losing libido, as the rest of us were losing money. Are there still people who think money and sex are not the same? Girlfriends of married men were having an especially hard time. One reported feeling shortchanged when her boyfriend explained that with the downturn his wife had started checking the bills. As for marriage to a banker, explained one young woman on the very funny blog *Dating a Banker Anonymous* ("free from the scrutiny of feminists"), "This recession has just bought everyone an extra two years of the single life." Another wrote that "this whole messy ordeal has advanced my Botox start date by at least two years."[5]

A month further into tough times, there were stories of a surge in the sale of home safes, but you need to spend big if you want a safe safe. "The worst thing a person can do is take all their valuables and put them in a lousy box," said a salesman at the store Megasafe in New Jersey. What you need is a safe meeting the TRTL-60XC standard, which means that a team of safecrackers using oxyacetylene torches cannot penetrate any of its six sides within an hour. Thus, as it gets harder to spend uselessly, as it gets harder to do the *depense* thing, you can at least make a final splurge and get a superexpensive box to hold your cash and jewels—like the $4,000 "Chinese Red" safe bought by a Manhattan businesswoman, reported as saying, "In these times, I feel I need something in my home." She also liked the red color. "If you can afford it, it's nice to walk into your house and see something that's not dull steel and gray. It's gorgeous. It's a beautiful piece."[6]

After all, on the cover of the September 2009 issue of *Vogue*, red was pronounced *the* color for fall. The notoriously power-driven editor, Anna Wintour, queen of the world's fashion (featured in R. J. Cutler's documentary *The September Issue*, and thinly disguised as an ace bitch in the movie *The Devil Wears Prada*), put the *depense* thing well when she wrote in her "Editor's Letter" that "although the current trend is towards the pragmatic and the accessible"—meaning cheaper, because of the world recession—"*Vogue* has a responsibility to fly a visionary flag, now more than ever." Not even Bataille could have put it as well, though he would have wondered how visionary you can get if you feel it is a responsibility. By the same token it is worth noting that *Vogue* (an inch thick and several pounds in weight) makes it difficult, if not impossible, to distinguish between advertisements and editorial content, its glossy pages, most not even numbered, blending in a delirious swirl of commerce and beauty—a riot of *depense*.

Now more than ever. In fact, adversity helps Wintour define what is at stake in fashion. Taking as her example the gorgeous fantasia of Little Red Riding Hood, dreamed up by *Vogue*'s creative editor, Grace Codrington, for the issue, Wintour deftly remarks that it keeps "fashion in the world of dreams and impossibilities."

The logic of *depense* is such that even if you try not to spend, that too can amount to *depense*. Take the prominent Manhattan realtor who declared her intent to stop riding around in the chauffered Rolls-Royce she rents because now, with the recession gathering force, it makes her deeply uncomfortable, so uncomfortable that she may downgrade to an Audi station wagon and keep the Rolls in a parking garage, swallowing the considerable cost of renting it because she is locked into a long-term contract. Thus, she "may end up paying handsomely for the privilege of looking thrifty."[7]

Yet as she took one of her last rides in the Rolls, according to the news story, two middle-aged women on the corner of Fifty-Ninth Street and Madison Avenue smiled broadly at the car, poking each other in glee. "They didn't look like they resented the passenger," writes the journalist. "They looked like the sighting had made their day, as if they'd spotted a rare and delightful bird in flight."[8]

Here in a nutshell we have the paradoxes peculiar to *depense*—first the luxury of the Rolls, then the luxury of hiding and not using it, and then the unmitigated love of seeing it, described in poetic language that would have enchanted Bataille: "the sighting had made their day, as if they'd spotted a rare and delightful bird in flight."

winnypoo

A RARE AND DELIGHTFUL BIRD IN FLIGHT. But the greatest example of *depense* in the mighty economy of the USA is the crisis itself, lurching in early 2009 from one extreme to another, one scandal to the next, one multibillion-dollar stimulus package after another intended, among other things, to get people to step up to the plate and spend once again as the almighty Deficit reaches astronomical levels and then some. This apocalyptic mix was nicely caught by a *New Yorker* cover in January 2009, showing a barefoot, bearded, long-haired man dressed in a smock, reminiscent of an Old Testament prophet, walking determinedly back and forth in front of an elegant store window like you find on Fifth Avenue in Manhattan, in which is displayed an expensive dress and a matching pair of women's shoes. He is clutching a gray sign on which, in yellow letters, is scrawled

THE END
IS NEAR
SALE

Birds in flight. Now tragic figures come to light in America. In California's once lush Central Valley, crops wither on the vine, the earth cracks from drought, the economy has fled, and the unemployment rate, the worst in the country, is close to 30 percent. Who would have thought it possible! But the people who come to Nima's beauty salon in my home away from home in a plantation town in Colombia have been living with 30 percent unemployment for decades, if not longer, ever since agribusiness swept into town in the 1950s and put an end to the era since the end of slavery, in 1851, in which people had their own small farms.

By the banks of the Paila River, not far from Nima's salon, lie heaps of refuse. White plastic bags float and play like low-flying birds. I see Gabriel, a stocky young cowherd, extracting with difficulty such a bag from the mouth of a cow. The bags block the intestines, he tells me. Can you imagine this? In years past shepherds and cowherds played their flutes in the shade of yonder tree, measured time by the passage of the sun, and worried about wolves and rustlers. Now their main concern is plastic bags! Only fifteen years ago there were no plastic bags. People used the leaves of plantain trees, or *viaow*, to wrap anything perishable. Of course, you will say, plastic bags are cheap and practical, but then you would have to explain why everything purchased—and I mean *everything*, from a pencil to a pork chop—is bagged as automatically as one inhales and exhales. Is this not a classic instance of good old *depense*, a little bit of *everyday wasting* with which to gladden our tepid souls, like wrapping pretty paper around a birthday present or El Mexicano's golden refuse?

Witness, then, the biblical scene: young Gabriel wrestling both bag and cow out there in the field. It is as if fate itself arranged this spectacle for the edification of mankind, struggling not with nature but with culture in the unwieldy shape of a plastic bag disappearing down the throat of a cow. But nobody notices it except me, a stranger who returns once a year. It is a wasted performance. *Depense* of *depense*.

And consider the degradation of the environment caused by chemicals in the river from the paper factory upstream, not to mention the megatons of pesticides, fertilizer, and hormones poured onto the insatiable sugarcane fields of the rich white guys who provide ethanol for automobiles! What devastating *depense* is this, wasting in a few decades the fantastically fertile black topsoil, not inches but meters thick, that took millennia to form.

The soil itself is the waste product of prehistory, *depense* on a cosmic scale. Let me emphasize the waste and wasting, nature's carnival, as volcanoes vomited out their insides high on the mountain ridges on both sides of the valley. Orgies of fire spewed ash rich in hot minerals that must have scored the skies black and red, then floated down into the meandering watercourses, swamps, and oxbow lakes of the valley floor, building up the precious topsoil that before the Spanish conquest kept the Indians happy, fishing and hunting as the waters receded. Today the river lies dammed and harnessed for the benefit of agribusinessmen with their pot bellies and shifty eyes, whose hands have never held—nor ever will—a machete or a shovel. *Pacora* is the name of the cane-cutting machete, extra long with a flared tip like a hammerhead shark, sharpened on all three sides. The agronomist Jorgé Giraldo tells me that studies show that a cane cutter swings his arm, on average, two thousand times a day to cut five to six tons of cane, something you may or may not care to think about with your next spoonful of sugar, bottle of Pepsi, or biofueled mile on the road. Then consider the burning heat, being clothed from head to toe in thick covering to stop the itch from the cane. The intense boredom. But not to worry. Too much. The owners of those swinging arms are on the way out; they are being replaced by expensive imported machines. What will they do now, these arms? Work was terrible. Being without work is worse. *Depense* on a grand scale, the men drift ever further into the interstices of slums and crime, their children, cognizant of the hopeless situation, long since headed in that direction.

With the creation of huge sugarcane plantations in the 1960s, buying out the peasant smallholders and their tree-based agriculture, the prehistoric rain of ash returned but in a new form. Today the skies fill daily with black ash from fields set afire when the sugarcane is ready to be harvested. Sugarcane has a lot of broadleaf underbrush. Up to ten years ago this was cleared by hand by the man cutting the cane. Now, to reduce the number of workers, the owners of the plantations burn the fields a day or two before harvesting, eliminating much of the underbrush but also releasing vast amounts of CO_2 into the atmosphere. Because seasonal variation is muted here close to the equator, sugarcane is planted year round and hence there are always fields being harvested. The fields roar red. Plumes of smoke rise into the sky like the volcanoes must have done and, with a majestic calm belying its furious origins, black ash floats down on the towns, into washtubs, onto laundry hung out to dry, onto the streets through which we walk, and into the air we breathe.

As I said, *depense* on a cosmic scale, ancient and modern, combined with the very opposite of *depense*—a dreary uniformity, a sterility of the imagination so immense that it amounts to another manifestation of wild extremity—the endless all-the-same cane fields stretching, it seems, forever, with a rectlinearity so forbiddingly unnatural that all prospects for life—human as well as that of plants other than the chemically sustained sugarcane—seem as flattened as the land itself. Everything is the same, hard and unrelenting sameness coated in dust, rampant with sadness and fear. I rarely see birds or small animals here. It is difficult to conceive of a living entity being so anti-life. No wonder I used to hear stories of the devil in the cane fields. But that was then. Now it's too tough even for him. I once heard a visitor to Colombia saying that you could get lost in a cane field and never find your way out, as it grows way over one's head and is very dense. This is an exaggeration, no doubt, but I remember the statement because it establishes the poetic reality of incarceration, of a labyrinth that is physical and economic and political and from which there is no escape. Not a human or house in sight. Stillness, silence, and the burning sun above. Gone are the peasant homes in the cacao groves with their rampant heterogeneity of life-forms, the norm here until the 1960s, a tree agriculture of cacao, coffee, plantains, and citrus, replicating the tropical rain forest.

What I am trying to say is that just as there is an aesthetic to clothes and the human body, which is very much the object of my inquiry here, is there not also an aesthetic in the way land is worked? I ask myself why we do not see this, why we restrict aesthetics to a sphere we call culture or a sphere we call consumption and hold these spheres to be separable from economics, forgetting the culture in agri-culture? The Trobrianders could never do that with their yam production, nor the Nuer with their cattle, and while it is obvious that capitalism has changed the rules of the game, alienating work and nature, that does not mean that even huge economic enterprises and even the most pragmatic decisions are not guided by aesthetic preferences like "bigger is better" or that there is not a moral imperative to cut down trees or become a car-borne culture eating Big Macs at fast-food chains under Golden Arches.

Surely this is not the only way to make money or to eat. It is not economic necessity or the need for profit that forces this particular mode of life upon the modern world, is it? There are many ways of making something, small or large-scale, just as there are many ways of consuming, and each way has its own picture, its own story, and its own style. What a shock to come across a chapter in Frazer's

Golden Bough, "The Worship of Trees." The clear-cutting by the sugar plantations of the trees that had formed traditional peasant farming, so as to enforce in the tropics the agribusiness model of North American and European open-field agri-culture, is as much a colonial imitiation and an aesthetic vote as it is the result of scientific and economic calculation. Small is no longer beautiful. Cosmic sugery was practiced on the Colombian landscape long before it was carried out on the bodies of Colombian women.

The technical is always already aesthetic. The "readymades" of Marcel Duchamp make this point. A coat rack, a shovel, a urinal—all are works of art as much as useful technology. People have interpreted Duchamp's Dadaism as a spoof of art and aesthetics. But that is to miss the critique in his work of the assumption that utility, technology, and economics are separable from art and aesthetics. (Note the use of the word "work," as in artwork) The modern meanings of "the economic" may have blinded us to these connections, but the older, classical meaing of this ancient Greek word, *oeconomia*, meaning the art (poesis) of householding, gets it right. What is still today meant by craft is the same in this regard, for in craft the technical is no less aesthetic than the aesthetic is a question of technique. Take Shaker furniture, for example. Nor is sensitivity to magic and the role of spirits likely to go amiss, as we find manifest in the work of blacksmiths in Africa or glassblowers in Herat, Afghanistan, and latent, I would hazard, with crafts elsewhere, as well as in the craft of sports such as basketball and with actors in the theater. "Break a leg," they say as you go on stage. The Trobriand and Nuer economies are exemplary, as is the following description of a young meteorologist drawing up his daily weather chart early in the morning in San Francisco in the late 1930s. Being young and trendy he thinks of weather as a branch of physics, and unlike his wily elders, who have a gut feel for weather, he loves applying complex equations to data sent in by ships at sea and from control stations across the United States, equations that concern velocities and accelerations, Coriolis force, and frictionless horizontal rectilinear flow. "To a well trained mathematical meteorologist," writes George R. Stewart in his novel *Storm*, "they were more beautiful than Grecian urns."[1]

Aesthetics extends way beyond Nima's beauty parlor, where I get my hair cut. I think of her place as a microcosm, an atelier for the production and conservation of beauty. Yet as with one's hair, so with Wittgenstein's "forms of life" extending into society at large. Another such atelier is the cemetery, a few blocks from Nima's salon, where Raúl paused at the grave of a seventy-year-old man and in his droll way explained to me that the man was found naked and dead due to a cerebral thrombosis caused by Viagra while making love to a young woman. "He was complaining of a headache," she said. The way Raúl described this made it seem that the naked man was found in the cemetery itself, and for several months I carried that picture around in my head. Maybe he was? In my mind's eye I see them, the naked old man and the young woman making out by the gravestones, the quintessence of beauty and the beast, love and death wrapped in each other's embrace. Even young guys are now taking Viagra to keep a hard-on, Raúl says. Another beauty and the beast story. In fact a whole bunch of them.

The light in the street between the beauty salon and the cemetery was a pink plastic sheen emanating from tiny storefronts with names painted in English like "Baby Shower." Between two stores sat a slinky girl on a red plastic chair showing a lot of leg. Next to her a yellow sign in Spanish:

BIG PARTY TONIGHT
RAFFLE OF A BEAUTIFUL WOMAN AND A JUG OF AGUARDIENTE

Bataille says *exuberance is beauty*. There must have been a good deal of that in the graveyard. But can't we turn this around and say *beauty is exuberance*? That would put us back in Nima's salon a few blocks from the cemetery.

The cemetery. What an archive! In that same town in that same year Luz Marina told me of a neighbor, aged twenty-three, who was killed and cut into pieces, probably by a power saw. I hear her voice distinctly as I write this. She always speaks deliberately. "They had to open up his grave and coffin three times," she said, "to replace body parts. The killers came in cars and took him to Las Brisas out in the countryside, where people heard his cries. He was a *delincuente*. This was revenge."

It is a sign of the callousness that develops—Oh, so quickly it develops!—that I am more amazed at the repeated opening of the grave and coffin to add more body parts than I am at the rest of the story. It is the "detail" that makes everything else catch fire. In Bataille's terminology this is *depense,* the "extra" (as are the body parts themselves) that takes the already over-the-top story completely over the top, just as it is the mix of horror and pragmatism that takes your breath away—"breath" as in soul—to God knows where. And why is it, I ask myself, that in listening to and repeating this story of terror I fail to see that this too is as much an aesthetic, a work of art, as the actions and events related? Thus they merge, the beauty salon and the cemetery.

Two weeks later in the city of Medellin, eight o'clock at night, I stood outside a downtown shelter for homeless people driven from the countryside by paramilitaries. It is a busy intersection at which prostitutes gather. One, wearing a black and white tartan miniskirt, is six feet tall and beautiful. She, if she is a she, lifts the back of her skirt, places her hands on her naked buttocks, and bounces them rhythmically up and down as cars and buses roar past. Compare this with the other end of the female prostitute spectrum, faces knocked asymmetric by drugs and blows of misfortune. A young girl, about eighteen, stands there shuffling in slipperlike shoes, visibly pregnant, wearing dirty knee-length pants, elevated shirt exposing much belly.

Inside the homeless shelter I meet some newly arrived refugees. They are from the countryside around a town called Concordia in the southwest of the state of Antioqua, of which Medellin is the capital. This is their first night in the shelter. They are on the run, a family of seven: five children, ages four to eleven; their mother, Fatima, young with only a few teeth; and Edwin, the father, wearing a shiny blue and gold football shirt. The youngest is Camila, but everyone calls her *La Reina,* the Queen. They have a small room to themselves, dimly lit, a dark parquet floor, with a bunk bed. There is an acrid odor of urine. They are a jolly crew and smile and joke a lot. Only in Colombia, I say to myself. Only in Colombia do I find people who can laugh in the face of disaster. I wonder if Bataille would include that as *depense?* I would. Laughter like that is useless expenditure in its full glory.

They had worked as day laborers picking coffee when the harvest was on, father and mother working together, kids in tow, for seven dollars a day, depending how much they picked. After the harvest the father found what work he could for four dollars a day. I am using the past tense because I can't see them leaving the city or going

back to Concordia. Note the fateful name. Anything but Concordia. Tomorrow, says Edwin, he is hitting the streets to sell chewing gum.

Paramilitaries, they explain, came to their home to force Edwin to join them. They fled the next day, bringing their clothes, a red television, and four teddy bears—three small ones about six inches high and *un osso grande* about a foot high called Winnypoo, with yellow fur and red and blue clothes.

Useless expenditure? *Depense?* Surely not! Not Winnypoo! Not the TV—the *red* TV! Are these not the crown jewels of this fugitive family? Does not the entire and piquant value of the bears and the television lie in the fact that they are useless, the luxuries without which life founders? Of course, Winnypoo and the three little *ossos* and the red TV provide comfort and security in a savage world and are therefore useful. Following the same logic, one might say that Edwin's shiny blue and gold football shirt is useful. But they are useful only to the extent that they are not useful.

To call the bears and the TV luxuries, and thus put them into the same category as El Mexicano's luxuries, would seem a monstrous equation. Moreover it is El Mexicano and people like him who, supported surreptitiously by the police and the army, amass luxuries by forcing people like Fatima and Edwin and their five kids to flee. El Mexicano's gold-embossed toilet paper is derived from this violence. As he defecates, as he strains at stool, his body must mimic the violence out there in Concordia, where he shits all over people and the land. But then his eye catches on the four cleansing initials—JGRG—and he scrapes the slate clean.

How could one possibly compare a sweet little Winnypoo with the gold-embossed paper El Mexicano uses to wipe his bottom other than by the cruel logic of real-life fairy tales of beauty and the beast?

spending

UNTIL RECENTLY CAPITALISM HAS HAD a fraught experience with madcap spending and luxury, suppressing this wilder part of our nature in the name of utility and a penny-pinching mentality. I was born in 1940 in Australia. During my childhood and for much of my adult life in England, Colombia, and the United States, I would say that capitalism—or, more generally, "economics"—for me meant production, as in steel mills, coal mines, textile factories, and agriculture, combined with a tight rein on personal spending (bad), which was deemed the opposite of investment (good). Spending other than on "necessities" was an under-the-counter transaction with the world. It was something people did to get over a broken love affair or to celebrate something special, like New Year's or a winning bet on the horse races. It was therapy. It was painting the town red. Like war, it filled a place previously occupied by carnival and magic. Otherwise it was guilt.

Spending when one should have invested was what working-class people (and, even more, the lumpen proletariat) supposedly did because they didn't have the middle-class ethic of saving for a rainy day. Incapable of restraint, drinking and gambling and whoring and buying stuff as soon as they had a penny or two in their pockets, if they had pockets, these Great Spenders and Wasters plagued the Western imagination until the end of World War II, when spending, meaning "consumerism," became a wonderfully good and ennobling thing, a civilizing uplift like a new religion, as when, a decade later, an Austrian architect and socialist by the name of Victor Gruen designed what is said to be the world's first shopping mall, located outside Minneapolis, Minnesota. "The merchants will save civilization" was one of his more memorable insights. Years later, disappointed that his concept of the mall did not in practice function like Ye Olde Village Square, Gruen returned in disgust to Vienna, denouncing the mall as nothing more than a big box in a sea of parking. "Gigantic shopping machines," he called them, leaving it to the US president in the wake of 9/11 to tell Americans to restore normalcy by shopping in these machines, which now exist worldwide, very much including the cities of what used to be called the third world.

If the invention of the credit card was a milestone in this history, so was that of the Welfare Queen, the two together presenting the Grand Dilemma: the urge on the one hand to foment a spending culture, on the other to restrict that culture to the responsible and deserving members of society, honestly working at honest jobs and not sucking the teat of the welfare state, reserved for bailouts of the superrich. How intertwined and comic these distinctions became is now manifest with the soaring US deficit and the impossibility of bringing it down without stopping spending, which would hamper the consumer's ability to get the economy back on track through the use of what the experts call "consumer muscle." With this telling phrase we see how the revolution is now complete. *Consumption* has become *production*, or at least "muscular," the last gasp of the Protestant ethic, unable to encompass the brilliance of spending for its own sake, which is actually what is driving the disaster, whether on the *depense*-inspired battlefields of US wars or in the shopping malls and eBay.

So what exactly is the "consumer"?

This new post-World War II creature actually entails a far older, indeed primeval, being, who seems already to have existed deep in the imagination of society, as in the picture which that indefatigable chronicler of the London poor, Henry Mayhew, created of the vagabonds of the mid-nineteenth century, a class of people whom he thought could be found pretty much any place at any time, whether on the High Veldt of southern Africa, hanging around the camps and villages of the more settled indigenous people, or in the capitals of Europe. Small wonder he called them "the wandering tribes." They had pronounced jaws and cheekbones and small heads together with a large muscle mass that diverted blood from their brains, a secret language, *cuze-cut* or slang, a repugnance to regular and continuous labor, a passion for stupefying herbs and roots as well as intoxicating liquors, insensibility to pain, immoderate love of gambling, a love of libidinous dances, pleasure at witnessing the suffering of sentient creatures, delight in sports and warfare, love of vengeance, a loose concept of property, an absence of chastity among the women, and but a vague sense of religion.[1]

This list, to my way of thinking, applies pretty much to the aristocrat as well—the repugnance to labor, the passion for liquor, and, of course, the immoderate love of gambling, sports, and warfare—all testimony to the immoderate spending that Bataille called *depense*. The primitive and the aristocrat share a deep bond as connoisseurs of *depense*, the grand art of wasting.

Then there is that other wandering tribe—today's teenagers. Is not the history of the world the history of the family? When my children were around seven years old, and more so in their teenage years in the early 1990s, the psychic orientation of the individual, as well as the national and international economic culture, changed fundamentally. My symbols of progress had been steel mills, penicillin, automobiles, and freeway construction. Now it was Nike shoes, Timberland boots, baseball caps, video games, Walkmans, special T-shirts, and windbreakers. And what didn't the kids know about drugs, over-the-counter as much as under? Everyman became a walking pharmacopeia. That, my friend, is what you call real *depense*, for which "drugs" was just a jaded euphemism.

When I was a kid in Australia in the 1940s, the economy meant sheep and the hard-working wheat farmer. Today the economy means looting the entire island for coal to export to China, digging deep and wide until it seems nothing will be left but a thin shell of sandy soil, as Australians get richer and richer so they can buy stuff made in China. Didn't the kids always say that if you dug a deep enough hole you would end up in China? Long forgotten are the bleating sheep running in circles and the penurious wheat farmers, symbols of a sweaty nation once dedicated to work instead of spending. They say Australia has now the largest houses in the world. I'm not surprised. They say there is enough coal for centuries but that once it has all been excavated and Australia is a big hole, then the countries to whom its plentiful deposits of uranium ore were sold will pay to have Australia take back the spent ore, to fill the hole with radioactive waste. Bataille's case studies of *depense*—Aztec sacrifice, potlatch on the Northwest coast, Tibetan theocracy, and so forth—pale before this little gem.

All this was predicted by my childhood favorite, *The Magic Pudding*, written and illustrated by the painter Norman Lindsay, who lived in the Blue Mountains outside of Sydney in the 1920s. It was the story of a pudding possessed of fast legs, a nimble mind, and a marvelous magic. For no matter how much of this delicious pudding was eaten, it would replenish itself full to the brim, a nice example of how Bataille's general economy relies on the child's imagination or, should I say, the adult's imagination of the child's imagination.[2]

Meanwhile in the USA, as elsewhere in the brave new world of Thatcher-Reagan, freed from government regulation, Wall Street was on the same cocaine-driven curve as Mayhew's wandering tribe, gambling on unheard-of riskier than risky loans, urging the avaricious, if not the needy, to *depense* a little more and take out mortgages on houses they could not afford. The middle-class home in the suburbs, which used to have one bathroom, expanded from the 1960s onward; by the 1990s its obligatory two children and a dog were housed in palaces so grand that the spaces rang with loneliness. The connection to the rest of the world was through the double garage, not the front door. And as the cars that drove you right into your house got bigger and bigger, approaching the size of a house, so the glass of their windows got darker and darker. What were they afraid of? Bataille is here, there, and everywhere, holding his sides with laughter when not screaming, "I told you so!"

Coincident with this supersizing and vanishing behind dark glass, the house got cut off from the ever more anonymous street. Front porches became a thing of the past. Heaven forbid that people would sit outside late on a hot afternoon and greet the neighbors Norman Rockwell-style! Now they had air conditioning and a visceral distaste for, if not fear of, other people. It became so much easier to spend life inside, buying stuff online and cozying up to what you bought. "Inside" came to be defined and experienced as an insatiable vortex of ever-expanding nothingness, as other sorts of people, the ones who did not have monster homes with treadmills and fat-free milk, grew fatter and fatter and fatter still as the worldwide epidemic of diabetes and hypertension spread its capacious self. In the inner city of the so-called developed world (now there's a word for you) and in the cities of the third world, barred doors and windows and broken glass on the tops of walls, along with killer watchdogs, displayed the reality of our new ways of life dedicated to consummation through consumption. And they wonder why kids turn to drugs. "Let it rip. Spend. Spend. Spend." Hearken to the gnome they loved, that state-defined oracle, Alan Greenspan, who dutifully served four US presidents from the Great Communicator onward. You would have been hard put to spot the difference between Native American-owned casinos and Wall Street, except that the former steadily made money, while the Wall Streeters and Greenwich, Connecticut, hedge-funders needed the US government to bail them out when their firms (a strange word in this context) went belly up. So-called pyramid schemes and Ponzi schemes flourished the world over, if only to make it look as though ordinary, day-to-day capitalism was not itself, at its core, a gigantic Ponzi scheme, bound for self-destruction, bailouts, and Christmas presents for the bankers.

In the same vein, blue jeans were no longer for labor—heaven forbid! A pair from the designer Christophe Decarnin of Balmain cost $10,000. Gucci's relatively downmarket version, at $396, comes already faded, as if from long tiring days in the hot sun, setting fence posts or driving cattle (not that cattle are driven anywhere anymore), and the cowboys are fakes or, worse, fakes of fakes. This move from work to fashion, from utility to flair, sums up the shift in world history that I am trying to depict.

But is this really all that new? Maybe this mighty history is only a chapter, perhaps the last one, in a more inclusive history in which production was a diversion, almost an accident, and nothing more than a means to an end, meaning spending. Marshall Sahlins has well described "the original affluent society" of (mere) hunters and gatherers with their digging sticks, bows and arrows, wicker baskets—and stacks of time for ritual, feasting, and lolling around.[3] His point is that scarcity is not the mark of so-called primitive society but instead of so-called affluent society, where, as the craze to consume spreads ever wider, enabling capitalist growth, so does the feeling that one never has enough, combined with the even greater feeling of having to consume more.

Thus does Marx's rewriting of Hegel's *Philosophy of History*, from ancient Greece and Rome, through the Middle Ages, into full-blown industrial capitalism, require a shift in emphasis. How poignant yet how misleading is Marx's fixation on production, as with his observation that only with modern capitalism does production become the aim of man, displacing prior epochs in which man was the aim of production. He got the alienation right, wherein man becomes a cipher in a profit/efficiency equation, but he lacked a theory of "consumption" and his idea of "man" perforce remained an abstraction unable to contemplate the wilder sides of that alienation. Man is now very much the "the aim of production," even if it is not quite the man Marx had in mind.

"The general aspect of life is *not* hunger and distress, but rather wealth, luxury, even absurd prodigality," wrote Nietzsche at roughly the same time Mayhew and Marx were analyzing the wandering tribe, and we will have ample reason to return to this.[4] For those of us coming out of a long and stormy tradition that yoked production to distress as the way to comprehend history ("history from below"), it is shocking to see all of that set aside as so much pious fluff, conventional Christian piety, and in its place find "absurd prodigality" as the motor of history, no time more so than today.

cool

AMAZINGLY ENOUGH, THIS SAME MOVE from production to consumption and from work to fashion has meant that Henry Mayhew's "wandering tribe" of dissolute consumers at the bottom of
society—without work and dangerous in the eyes of the gainfully
employed—have these past few years been closely studied by fashion
designers for style trends to sell to the affluent. No doubt fashions at
the bottom of the social pyramid have been copied by the well-to-do
for many a year, but it is hard to believe that the systematic and intensive study of such elements existed before consumption became
an industry (now, if that's not a strange phrase!).

Today the fashions of the wandering tribe don't percolate upward
unassisted. Take the *L Report*. As described by *New Yorker* staff writer
Malcolm Gladwell in 1997, two women put the *L Report* together every six months, and there is something wonderfully obscene in what
they do—in their shameless but ever so cool mix of anthropology,
surveillance, empathy, spying, and manipulation, inveigling teenagers in the ghetto to tell them what's cool. Reporting on what the
kids are wearing to help fashion houses keep ahead of the game, the
authors of the *L Report* inform us that "today's consumers, regardless of age or income, aspire to style and prestige like never before."[1]

Like never before. Especially beguiling is their claim that their "data
comes from an exclusive network of Urban Pioneers in style and
prestige across the globe." To read this is to feel instantly of the moment—to be at the burning tip of fashion, and also to be embraced
by an elite corps spread worldwide, like the Knights of Malta, the
Masons fussing with their aprons, or some other secret sacred sect

such as the terrorists we are always being warned against, depicted with bravura in our mainstream movie worlds. Could it be that the thrill of fashion is itself a fundamental aspect of terror?

I mean who *are* these "Urban Pioneers"? Surely we have met them before with the wandering tribes of Mayhew's London or the visions of North American Indians that animate the Paris we find in the stories of Balzac, Hugo, and Dumas? Baudelaire's poems founded the poetry of *apachedom*, a genre that lasted at least eighty years.[2] But as the sublime of the lonely forests and deserts gave way to the pulse of the inner city, so fashion has found its wandering tribe in the ghettoes of New York, Los Angeles, and Chicago.

There is one question in particular that intrigues me about this trickle-up fashion pump, and that is why it concerns only the boys and not the girls in the 'hood? The phantasm of male virility (sex and crime) seems intrinsic to this fashion pump, disobeying the laws of gravity and much else beside. In Gladwell's eleven silky pages on cool written for the decidedly uncool demographic of people who read the *New Yorker* (talk about trickle-up! John Updike's sagas of the upper-middle-class white suburbs define the magazine), there is not one—*not one*—mention of a girl, except, of course, the two blonde women from Connecticut, who seem to be doing rather well, diving into the ghetto to see wassup stylewise, then having others get it copied posthaste in sweatshops across the globe before they come out with their next biannual catalog—priced, in 1997, at $20,000 a copy.

If girls do appear it is to be appropriated by boys, as when we accompany Gladwell as he accompanies a coolhunter to the Bronx (note the word *hunt* here; we really are in the jungle). She hands a homeboy there a new shoe, the Reebok DMX RXT, *meant for girls*, and the homeboy loves it. This makes the coolhunter very excited. It's not everyday that one can provoke and witness so much raw cool. The *New Yorker* loves it too, presenting a full-page illustration of the shoe by Filip Pagowski, shown suspended overhead, sole in our faces, flaring in a maelstrom of color—a perfect visual metaphor for the trickle-up fashion pump pumping cool from the 'hood to the elevated spheres of society. The shoe looks alive. It really is a kick-ass shoe, like a seven-league boot lifing itself by its own bootstraps. Not a human being in sight, just the shoe hurtling through space like that "rare and wonderful bird in flight."

Faced with the starburst of color emanating from the shoe's sole

Reebok's DMX RXT didn't hit as a girl's shoe, but boys in the Bronx call it butter.

Drawing by Filip Pagowski. From Malcolm Gladwell, "The Cool Hunt," *New Yorker*, March 17, 1997.

as it rises into the galaxy of heavenly being, faced with this clear evidence of the shoe as animated, magical, treasure-laden being, how might one weigh the claims made by Karl Marx and Sigmund Freud as to the fetish that, rather strangely, I must admit, seems inseparable from shoes? Of all things, shoes! For both Marx and Freud draw on a plenitude of shoe stories to make the point basic of their life's work, as if they were also *coolhunters* way ahead of the curve. Marx bases his economics on Aristotle's example of shoes for use versus shoes sold for profit in ancient Athens, and Freud tells us how shoes can be sexually potent because—in a now you see it, now you don't rhythm—they stand in for seeing and simultaneously not seeing a tabooed piece of anatomy, the absent phallus hidden in the genitalia of one's mother. A tall story, you say, yet how accurate is this on again, off again rhythm as regards fashion's moody changes of heart, lurching from one extreme to the next in the blink of an eye? It was all there, it seems to me, that excitement and that complexity, in the encounter in the shoe shop in the Bronx between the coolhunter and the homeboy aglow with enthusiasm for a girl's shoe.

But how does the shoe feel in all this? Is it not alive? Does it not have feelings and hopes? It is a fetish, after all. Does it not reciprocate being seen and not seen by displaying yet concealing itself? Thus does Freud's fetish merge with Marx's in *the artful display of not displaying*—which is the very basis of cool, to display, that is, but not (most definitely not!) to be seen doing such. This was the specialty and defining characteristic of the *dandy*, ambidextrously (i.e., ambipedally) located in world history, one foot in the market, the other without. To be cool is to surf the fetish, the sexual fetish as well as that of the commodity, and hence to combine them. And if that sounds thrilling, just think what it must be like to be a coolhunter.

If you think Freud and Marx are in over their heads, what about Walter Benjamin, who in remarks from the 1930s seizes upon fashion as the *abracadabra*—the magically inspired throttle—of that noble engine of capitalism, the free market? Fashion is the death ritual of the commodity, he announces, and goes on to equate fashion with both sex and death, nowhere more so than when he writes that yesterday's fashion is a radical anti-aphrodisiac.[3]

This equation of sex and death with fashion is the same equation we come across in Frazer's *Golden Bough* concerning seasonal rhythms in the ancient worship of a great mother goddess who personifies the reproductive energies of nature. Only now nature has been given a decisive shove. It has been put through the wringer of the market, and those reproductive energies have been harnessed for profit—up to a point. Only up to a point. For there must always be a beyond profit, a beyond for the sake of beauty alone in all its glory, striven for but unattainable, and this is the beyond of fashion's far edge, where cool beckons.

We will return to this equation of sex, death, and fashion—it is after all the theme struck repeatedly in the grim stories peasant and working-class people tell me in Colombia about liposuction and cosmic surgery—but let me return for the moment—for fetishism is always of the moment and is always momentary on account of its flickering luster—let me return for the moment to *the image*.

It is no accident that the *New Yorker* would make an image of a shoe—*the* shoe, the *singular* shoe ("How cool is that!" you can hear them chuckling)—because the fetish is every bit as much image as it is thing. This point is made with much élan by Fredric Jameson in comparing Martin Heidegger's analysis of Van Gogh's painting of a pair of well-worn boots (1886) with Andy Warhol's sparkling picture of never-to-be-worn diamond-dust shoes arranged as in a shop-window display—singles, not pairs, and of many different colors, arranged as if randomly.[4] The contrast could not be more perfect. Van Gogh's boots—not shoes—are crumpled and worn with the travail of time and travail. Their plenitude—their authenticity, shall we say—is made manifest by the shadows that accumulate in the folds of the crumpled leather no less than in what can only be described as a halo of light on the floor behind them. Meanwhile Warhohl, the perfect artist for the new industry, the industry of consumption, makes every effort to render his glittering women's shoes as without depth and without any authenticity whatsoever. These shoes are fake, proudly and ostentatiously and lovingly so. Van Gogh's boots reek of history and labor and use. They become more useful and thus more valuable as they age and fit better into the world, the world of the foot and the world of the soil and roadways, while Warhol's little shoes, all asparkle, speak to our brave new world of spending—not history nor walking nor, heaven forbid, working—where only illusions are real and each of us can be a celebrity for one diamond-dust moment in our otherwise forgettable lives.

For no matter how material the appearance, it is appearance that matters. The fetish object is image at the same time as it is thing. Cool is a matter of things, that's for sure—shoes and shirts and pants and belts and hats, textures and materials and hair, the way the body is held and the way it moves, carving up space—yet it is also, and because of all that, predominantly image, predominantly the occasion of looking and being looked at, of display and observation but within an effervescent, ephemeral optical field, because the closer you get to cool, the more it hides. If you have to define it, you haven't got it. Ditto for fashion, a slightly less cool version of cool.

There is a terrible lesson here. He who would write on cool, or she who would make money out of cool, has to be preternaturally endowed with stability in the face of chaos. Cool is ruthless in its insistence on change. Gladwell and the *L Report* have long since been rolled over by cool, by the irresistible but unpredictable speed-up that is fashion, the six-month rhythm of 1997 now being reduced to six days, or so I am informed by people in the know. How they know is another story. And anarchy has struck like never before. There is no linear evolution, no trend that can help you predict what will be cool tomorrow. To the despair of the fashion houses and trendsetters awaiting the word from on high or down low, cool is like DJs mixing old musics. All one can do is limp behind, cruelly caught on camera with an E for effort instead of a C for cool.

The shift in world history from saving to spending is shadowed by a mighty shift in the importance of the visual image. We have in some fundamental sense become nothing but image. That is the meaning, the power, and the huge price of the *L Report* and all it stands for as *cool*. A new reckoning has been born, more virtual than real, even while the old reality lingers, it being the human body that combines the real with the superreal, while cosmic surgery provides the lifeline between the two, connecting real flesh to real image, the spending spree to vituality.

But to call this a *spending spree* misses the point. The term sounds old-fashioned, mired in a fuddy-duddy way of seeing things, as if the greater and more substantial reality were still a stable, authentic, prudent universe, punctuated by sporadic spurts of spending that soon die down, allowing the non-carnivalesque world to resume its role in defining the real—which, you will be pleased to hear, is not superficial and hollow at its core.

Dream on. Them days be over. The fairy-tale quality I discern in this major shift in world capitalism has to do with seduction by enchanted objects: diamond-dust shoes, the Reebok DMX RXT sneaker. The names tell it all—diamonds and diamond dust, side by side with the power-saw snarl of DMX RXT sneakers and the harsh consonantal gnashing of names like Reebok that empty out into the vacuity of that charmed space of every thing and no thing. This seduction by that space is what lies at the heart of the world's ever more frantic consumption, and at the heart of this heart lies one of the most enchanting objects of all—the human face and body—conniving with that magic of display we call cool, pumped out of the inner city.

There is only one thing more enchanting than beauty, and that is the capacity to metamorphose into beauty.

the designer smile

IT IS ONE THING TO RESHAPE a nose or a breast. It is quite another to reshape a smile. In "Surgeons of the Underworld," a September 2009 article following the capture of the drug trafficker Chupeta, a man subject to much cosmic surgery, the newspaper *El Tiempo* included two stories about a Bogotá dentist giving his paramilitary clients new smiles, as if that were like any other cosmic surgery.

But when it comes to one's smile I am struck by an ineffable radiation indicative of a new metaphysical core of personhood that a new nose, for example, would struggle to achieve. The word used is not "make" or even "create" but "design," as in "designer jeans." Surgeons and dentists do not merely make but rather design smiles—and while I can imagine restless nights spent figuring out one's ideal nose, I think it takes a good deal more cosmic tinkering to design a new smile, revelatory of the inner self illuminating the world.

One of the men sporting a designer smile, as illustrated in a photograph in *El Tiempo*, is none other than one of the stars of the Colombia paramilitary pack, Salvatore Mancuso, officially accused of at least eighty-six assassinations but in all likelihood responsible for many, many more. He is said to be the brains behind years of unspeakable terror in northern Colombia and as a result to be immensely wealthy. Allied with judges, senators, mayors, police, and the very highest ranking army officers—ties often rumored over the past fifteen years but only now confirmed, insofar as anything of this nature is ever "confirmed"—Mancuso had at the time of my writing taken up the government's generous offer to confess his sins (at least some of them) in return for retaining most of his wealth and serving a reduced sentence of four years in a nicely outfitted jail, with cell phones to keep tabs on his affairs.

Many people feel this process of confession and brief imprisonment is a charade that allows the government to feign doing something about the paramilitary terror machine to which it is in fact closely attached, a suspicion only enhanced when you see the photograph of Mancuso in Itaguí prison, close to Medellin, that appeared in a daily newspaper in August 2007. Dressed in a striped shirt of the latest fashion, a little paunchy around the jowls, Mancuso looks down submissively, hands together under his chin as if in prayer. Mouth partly open like a fish, he is about to say something but cannot. It's all too awful. He is a model of shame. The caption reads, "We were the mist, the smoke curtain, that hid everything."

The designer smile raises many questions, one being why good fortune has continued to smile on these paramilitary mass murderers. But there are more personal questions as well. Ask yourself what sort of smile you would like. Ask yourself if you have asked yourself this question, and ponder your reply. Wasn't your smile all but unknown to you but nevertheless what made you unique and glowingly alive and human for your friends on Facebook and the local shopkeepers? What does it mean to fiddle around with something as mysterious and fundamental as your smile?

Drawing his father's face when he died, John Berger tells us that as he sketched his mouth, his brows, and his eyelids, he felt the history and experience that had made them what they were.[1] What would Berger have felt if his father, like Mancuso, had had his smile replaced? What happens to history itself when the face is thus altered, especially when we gaze at it at death?

As regards the transfiguration of the face that accompanies one's smile, a transfiguration that spreads like magic to the faces around, it is intriguing to consider what Walter Benjamin writes of the connections between death and storytelling. At one point he suggests that when you die a natural death, not one moored to IV drips and monitors, a sequence of images is released from inside you, "unfolding views of yourself under which you encountered yourself without being aware of it." These images emerge and play out on your face, which becomes a screen for the movie now rolling as life winds down. For the people gathered around you this is an unforgettable moment, for this is the face that imparts authority to everything that concerned you and is thus, suggests Benjamin, the source of the storyteller's art.[2]

A bizarre idea, to be sure, but one that might make you think twice before changing your face, for what would happen then to the intricate mechanism, the unfolding sequence of images of self-encounters, and what might be the consequences for the art of storytelling, the glue that holds our lives together on this poor earth?

The ancient arts of physiognomy (discerning insides from outsides, reading the soul in the face) may seem like hocus-pocus today, but when you stop to think about it, you realize it is embedded in our everyday practice, such that you really have to wonder whether the fundamental reason for cosmic surgery is precisely to reverse this mechanism, to create a new inside by changing the outside.

And once we have gotten a new inside, fate itself will change, making this cosmic tinkering akin to alchemy and related magical practices. This is why cosmetic surgery is best considered cosmic surgery. Physiognomic manipulation aspires to be not simply a face-lift but a soul-lift. Cosmic surgery is nothing more than a gloss on a far more basic operation, the latest expression of ancient magical practices based on mimesis and physiognomy, practices such as masking, face painting, and body painting, carried out so as to greet the gods or become one.

Given the importance of the face as the mother and measure of all images, together with its role in storytelling and the complex sense of surface and depth, outsides and insides, you really have to wonder what would happen if a large number of faces were given designer smiles? Would this not impact decisively on what Baudelaire called "the correspondences"—that poetic network of signs and symbols that make up, or used to make up, our universe? It would be like a computer virus let loose in God's software. I gather that the People in Charge are mightily concerned about cyber attack taking out our electrical networks, water supplies, traffic lights, and so forth (the "next Pearl Harbor," according to CIA chief Leon Panetta). But when are they going to pay attention to the delirious potential of cosmic surgery playing havoc with our semiotic systems?

Once again the vernacular shows more sensitivity than the People

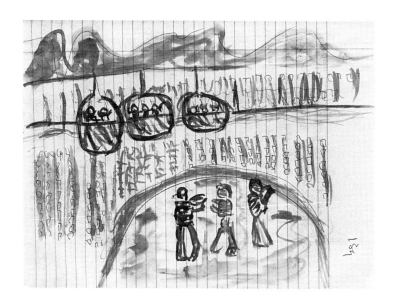

in Charge, as with the expression *cara y contra cara*—face and counterface, deception and counterdeception—which is how a young paramilitary, formerly an urban guerrilla fighter in Colombia's National Liberation Army (ELN), described this world of correspondences gone awry to me in a slum on a rainy mountainside overlooking Medellin in 2006. Swaying cable cars creaked overhead as we surveyed the city below. Windswept clouds clung to the mountains, from which mist was rising.

Here nobody could eavesdrop. It was a like a scene in a Hitchcock movie. The city spread out far below as we stood there alone, high on history. Only truth could percolate through these chill heights where the air is thin. Here we could see the big picture, *cara y contra cara,* while the cable cars glided above us bearing messages like those put in bottles thrown into the sea, as if that miracle of public-works engineering represented Nietzsche's eternal return, the whirring of secrets and tides. We were alone, listening to stories about the days when ELN gunmen controlled everything we saw below, until removed by the paramilitaries who now pretend to be disbanding and allow the government troops to pretend to take control. *Cara y contra cara.* As I write in February 2010, the killing in Medellin is off the charts as the paramilitaries now wage war on each other.

El Columbiano.

But real as all that is, it is but an allegory for a larger and denser reality: that for a long time now the state itself has existed as an exercise in extreme makeover, a cosmic surgeon's dreamscape in which the face is continuously being recreated to hide the other face, the face of paramilitary control from the lowest to the highest levels of government, and this to such an extent that it seems entirely warranted to see the largest body under the knife—the cosmic surgeon's knife—as the body of the nation-state itself, like Mancuso, receiving its designer smile.

the designer body

THE BODY OF THE NATION-STATE under the knife is the same body that Alberto the taxi driver transports, muffled and bound from neck to knee—"like a mummy," he says—in the back of his cab speeding from the clinic in Cali to the patient's home in a small town an hour south.

"90-60-90," he says, gesturing awkwardly to his breasts, waist, and buttocks (the figures being centimeters). "Oh, this makes for problems!" he sighs. "Because today women are vain. They all want to be beauty queens."

Vanity?

It was all rather strange. I mean, who isn't vain? Aren't men vain too—Salvatore Mancuso, for instance, with his "designer smile"? And why is vanity bad?

"Today they are vain." Not yesterday but *today*. By Alberto's account the rapidity of change is electrifying. *En Cali es enfermizo*, he said, *contagious*, like the plague, referring to the current craze for *la lipo* and breast enlargement. Women will prostitute themselves to get the money for this—it is said—inspired by the girlfriends of the *narcos* and the TV newscasters, almost always women with long blonde hair and the obligatory 90-60-90. With that body and hair, and the national anthem playing for them as part of the worship accorded such divinities at the mythologically strategic hours, 6-12-6, the nation-state is in excellent shape, even if most of its citizens are not.

The demand is insatiable. A young producer for *Cambio Extremo*, a Colombian TV show (based on the US show *Extreme Makeover*) that offers free cosmic surgery so as to radically alter a person, tells me that some twenty thousand volunteers responded to a single advertisement for surgery in Bogotá. Everyone will tell you that "beauty opens doors." The women in Congress, including the president of the senate and the new minister of foreign affairs in 2007 are stunningly glamorous. And when the politically progressive mayor of Medellin replaced the city's annual beauty contest with a contest for women of talent, they too seemed like beauty queens. One wonders what it takes to be a humble secretary, let alone the courtesan of a *narco*.

At times it seems that all the girls in Cali have been put to the knife, for it would be difficult to find in that city today young or middle-aged women without enlarged breasts, made all the more visible, or might I say, astounding, by their low necklines. Close by lies the city of Pereira, home of the recent best seller and TV drama *Sin tetas no hay paraiso*, which could be translated, awkwardly enough, as *Without (Artificially Augmented) Breasts, There Can Be No Paradise*. The most crushing disillusionment for a young Dutch militant, Tanja Nimeijer, member of the FARC guerrilla army, whose personal diary was found recently by the Colombian army, was that the girlfriends of the guerrilla commanders had breast implants and fancy lingerie. What happened to the revolution?

"The 800-pound gorilla in the room" is one of those tough-sounding, bullyboy expressions, equivalent to "the emperor's new clothes"—something highly visible but that nobody is able to acknowledge. In the Cali airport, and I dare say the same is true in Pereira, you could just as well evoke the "500 cc breasts" as that 800-pound gorilla. For these breasts remain, as far as I know, unmentioned and, who knows, virtually unseen, like the scotoma, or blind spot, to which Sigmund Freud drew our attention when describing seeing and simultaneously not seeing the mother's absent phallus. Fascinating consequences arise from this scotoma, amounting to what Freud at one point called the fetish, revealing and concealing the mysterious maternal organ to which I have just alluded (allusion itself being a matter of noting and not noting). This must be why Alberto referred so readily to the passengers packed in the back of his yellow taxi speeding home from the clinic as mummies—

mummies as in moms, with just the eyes showing above their bandaged bodies bouncing on the back seat.

To make matters still more confusing, Alberto and most everyone else with whom I talked were unembarrassed and matter-of-fact as regards this new topic of liposuction and cosmic surgery. Most times people were clinical and detached, while at other times they acted out the transformations, rippling their hands like waves down their bodies, strutting like beauty queens. Most everyone with whom I speak in Colombia now seems to be an expert on beautifying surgery, just as peasants on remote mountaintops or in impenetrable jungles now deftly open and fix their Nokia cell phones with a penknife, fingernail, or the tip of a machete. What I thought was something private and best left unsaid, the state of a person's breasts and sexual appeal, was actually a public secret known to all. Once the notion of *surgery* and the aura of *technology* were in the air, it seemed the nature of the conversation altered. Otherwise sacrosanct aspects of self were unwrapped in a jiffy. Could it be that as more attention is paid to the appearance of the body, to its aura and sex appeal, paradoxically the body becomes more of an object, a work of art, to be evaluated and discussed by everyone, acting like art critics or people discussing a soccer match, such that the older, sacred, tabooed qualities of the human body diminish or even disappear?

How precarious and subtle is this movement along the knife edge of taboo! In one moment, in one sphere of activity, nothing could be more shielded and hidden than the naked body. In another, as with these parodic evocations of surgically enhanced bodies, it is all "so yesterday" and unremarkable. Well, almost so. Are not these things a little too unremarkable? I think back to Daniella Gandolfo's remarkably unremarkable conversation in June 1996 with Mr. Morales, a photographer who was present in downtown Lima when an elderly street cleaner took off her blouse during a mass protest against firings of municipal workers. "No one dared touch her," Morales said. It seemed like the woman was in trance. She wandered around screaming unintelligble words. The police recoiled to the sidewalk. More women began to undress. It must have been on impulse, mused the photographer, like what happens in the mind of person when they commit suicide.[1]

All on account of a bared breast.

This seesawing on the taboo matches the movement back and

forth between sacred and profane. Take the small city of Pereira in central Colombia. Famous for its cosmic surgery, Pereira is also blessed with the reputation of being home to the best and best-looking whores in Colombia. But does this not present a problem? Do we not get to the nub of the issue concerning vanity and treating one's body as a showpiece when the first images that leap to mind are whores looking for a cheap fix? Actually, no. It does not present a problem, for what is happening here is not gradual acceptance of previously tabooed behavior so much as it is an acceleration of the back and forth between sacred and profane—as in the back seat of a taxi late one night in Bogotá, November 2011, fifteen years after the street cleaner took off her shirt in public in Lima. A mere eighteen inches from my eyes is a video showing, in vivid color, almost nude young women dancing to fast-paced music, the camera fixed on the mesmerizing spaces opened up between the dancers' legs. Can't shut it off. No way. The dark city flits past. And the driver has this same imagery playing on his instrument panel. Where are we going?

This same opening and closing of the Pandora's box of the female body was manifest in the newspaper *El Tiempo*, August 13, 2007, where six glamorous women, verging on middle age and in various forms of show business, apparently felt no qualms revealing secrets about their never-ending search for bodily perfection and the need to slow down, if not halt, the ravages of time, a search that involved repeated surgeries, often to correct earlier surgeries—of the breast, of the nose, of the smile, liposuction of the waist, facial stretching, elimination of cellulitis, toning of the skin, injections of Botox. Often what is required is a mere "touch-up," a *retoque*, of the ears, for instance, or a small liposuction, claims the celebrated Bogotá surgeon Gustavo Andrés Hincapié, who, as an aside, mentions that his patients include adolescents who come for breast augmentation. One forty-year-old actress says that in addition to surgery to enlarge her breasts, from 34 to 36B, she asked to have her nostrils closed a little. She constantly moisturizes her skin, she adds, and has frequent masages and injections of "mesotherapy," as well as Botox every six months. "For this you need an excellent doctor as your monitor." Another actress, Marabelle, has had eight operations this year alone (and we are only halfway into August), including surgeries to enlarge, then diminish, her breasts.

I am reading this in the heat of a wretched agribussness slum town, wondering what planet I live on. But then has not fashion swept us all into its whirlwind embrace, and has not cosmic surgery sculpting the female body become not only the foundation on which fashion deports itself but the ultimate sacrifice to the gods of fashion? Fashion used to be a discrete and minor affair, something for the back pages of the newspaper and weekend supplements. Fashion was nothing compared with the headlines concerned with drugs and guerrilla, paramilitaries and corruption, football and the exchange rate. But that was then.

My first day back in Colombia in 2009, the main newspaper, *El Tiempo,* carried alarming headlines on its first page concerning the imminence of war with Venezuela. That took up two columns. Next to that, but taking up three columns, was a color photograph of a barely clothed young woman aggressively displaying designer underwear at an annual lingerie fashion show in Medellin.

She glowered as if ready to take on anything the Venezuelans could deliver, her black "underwear" more like armor, a costume from *Star Wars,* accentuating the mostly naked breasts and thighs with some chain links begging to be undone. This is warfare in another key, and all the more delightful for not requiring tanks and guns. "Don't fuck with us" is what I read as the implied caption; bearing in mind Freud's play with "primal words," this means both "Please fuck me" and "I will fuck you," meaning destroy you. Seeing this model, with her mighty breasts and hands resolutely on her hips, you realized the country was in good hands. You could now relax and flip the pages of the newspaper to find the glossy magazine dedicated to "the most desired abdomens," with full-page color spreads of a naked young man, Gregorio Pernia, a Bogotá model, his hands pathetically serving as a fig leaf, making you wonder why photographs of naked men, but not of naked women, are invariably awkward.

In other words, the distinction between "news" and "entertainment" has come unstitched, not just as on Fox News, whose poisonous bilge and verbal vomit we have come to expect, but here in a sober and prestigious newspaper. Side by side with what surely amounts to some of the most serious news that can befall a nation, the threat of war with another sovereign state, we find soft porn. Has a mighty taboo fallen away, or has the game of transgressing the taboo become more complex? Under the excuse of fashion and on

ANESSA PELÁEZ lleva uno de los diseños que Tarra'o, empresa paisa especializada en ropa interior, presentó Colombiamoda, que finaliza hoy en Modollín. Dos iórigos di

El Tiempo, July 30, 2009.

the brink of war, the nation has become overtly sexualized, as befits a nation girding its loins. What used to be a minor media category, namely "fashion," now permeates not only everyday life but state-craft as well.

My seamstress friend Olivia Mostacilla, age fifty-eight, whose live-lihood has been ruined by the fashion industry and its cheap clothes from China, saw a close connection between the craze for liposuc-tion and the rise of fashion, especially pronounced now in Cali, with its famous designers and models from whom the lower ribs have been extracted to create a thinner waist, as God once did with Adam, for other reasons, setting fashion on its way. "It's everywhere!" she insisted, referring to cosmic surgery. "In whatever garage, with whatever nurse or whomsoever has taken a health course! It's the growth industry of Colombia! Any defect can be eliminated, any defect whatsoever. Virgins are remade. It was on the TV. You can do anything! Anything at all! All that is left of the person is their name!"

Always a step ahead of conscious awareness, fashion makes language race to keep up. How can I as writer and witness get across the pulsing energy of a craze? I recall when blue jeans were the most sought after item in Colombia in the late 1960s. North Americans in Cali were begged to sell their jeans—their used jeans—at phenomenal prices. Experts predicted a change worldwide in the human body, female and male, so as to fit into them. And they were right. Twenty years later *bluyinería* was a major source of income for enterprising, lower-class Colombian women around Cali, who, believe it or not, were then flying to Korea to buy jeans by the container.

Or Adidas and Nike sneakers! From the late 1980s on young people in the poor parts of town would, so it was said, literally kill to get a pair, real or fake, ripping them off the bleeding corpse. Thirty years earlier people were often barefoot. I mention this contrast not to explain the sudden mania for shoes among a previously shoeless population but to get across the speed of change and the forest-fire furor that fashion can attain as the hitherto unexplored continent of desire is breached, as the mummies wrapped from neck to knee in the back of Alberto's cab, speeding south from the liposuction clinics in Cali to this agribusiness town, bear witness.

You really pay your dues with *la lipo*. Right now Alberto is telling me in his droll, matter-of-fact way, of the woman he recently drove home. She is in a coma on account of *la lipo*. I cannot brush away images of darkness and pain in some airless room filling with waves of fear. Then a friend of mine for four decades tells me that his stepdaughter, Angela María, has been resting at home in the Cali slum of Aguablanca, recuperating for six weeks from a *lipo* of her shoulders, waist, and abdomen that cost twenty-five hundred dollars in Bogotá, where she works as a live-in maid. Her age? Twenty-seven. How could she possibly afford this on a maid's salary? And why? The pain is intense, he tells me, shaking his head. All this time she's lain in a tight corset to reduce swelling. She can't work and requires a special diet. "It recurs if you're not careful," he warns me. "Then you just get another *lipo!*" chimes in Robinson, aged all of fifteen. "Was she fat?" I ask bluntly. "No, Miguel. About the same as Anabeba here," replies my friend, pointing to his forty-five-year-old cousin, a strong peasant woman with a certain width, that's for sure, but not what I would call fat.

I call Angela María from the airport. "It was horrible," she says. She was madly swollen. The corset from her chin to mid-thigh has to stay on for two months. Like everyone I speak with, she emphasizes the high tech—the lab tests and clinical workup and the fact that the clinic was *recomendada*. "So why did you have the *lipo*?" I ask. "Because my friends are all thin and I wanted to be the same." What more can you say on the phone to a virtual stranger? What her voice conveyed, however, was invigorating, just what I would expect of a young woman from Aguablanca, although it was hard to imagine her resting much at home after I heard about the front door being stove in by young thieves who ran off with a pair of sneakers. What sickening irony. The same forces that led her to surrender her body to the fat vampire stove in her door to steal sneakers.

Are poor people as consumed now with being thin as the well-to-do? And to the extent that they are, does this not amount to a momentous change in the aesthetics at issue in class struggle and imitation? Let us think back to earlier epochs to consider this question and its implications. Let us think back no more than twenty years in Colombia. Did the peasants of the southern Cauca Valley, for instance, or of the Pacific coast, equate personal attraction with thinness then? Of course not. If anything, thinness was ugly and a sign of illness, perhaps sorcery.

And what of black people trying to become white? Does the new thinness amount to an imitation of what we might call a white body? I think it does. But I think there is reverse imitation as well. When I asked two black teenage schoolgirls in the countryside around Cali what they thought about *la lipo*, they responded by telling me about one of their teachers, a white women in her late twenties, who had had her butt made more prominent with implants. "You know," they explained with a giggle, "white women don't have much of an ass." Huge trailers carrying sugarcane rumbled past raising clouds of dust, sugarcane now grown on land that once belonged to Afro-Colombian peasant farmers, who are now forced to work for the plantations (if there is work). I thought how strange it might be for this teacher to stand every day writing on the blackboard in front of these schoolgirls, exhibiting her brand-new, Afro-inspired *pompis*—meaning butt. And if that is strange—a cross-ethnic mimesis, a divine hybrid—how much stranger these terms—*ass, butt, pompis*—words that pop out of the language to skate along the edge dividing the tabooed from the transgressive, the attractive from the repulsive, the humorous from the beautiful.

And my friend of several decades? I hadn't seen him in ten years and he had fallen on hard times, separated from his wife and unable to make anything but a miserable living as a deadbeat photographer in the slums of Cali. Instead of his fifty-five years he looked like a walking corpse, mere skin and bones, his eyes dark hollows with massive lids, cheekbones standing out, lips retracted over protruding teeth. This was that other "cosmic surgery," enacted by poverty. The other side of thinness.

Actually, this "other side" seems built into cosmic surgery. Countless times I am told of women having their breasts surgically enlarged, but then infection sets in and, horror of horrors, they need a double mastectomy. It is insistent, this story, the imagery grotesque, the punishment biblical. Something else is being expressed here, about something other than breasts. But then, what could be more mythic and more allegorical than a woman's breast?

Only the eyes, which are also enlarged by cosmic surgeons. A friend tells me of women who have had their eyes enlarged—and now can't close them.

"Imagine!" chimes in a neighbor, barely concealing a laugh. "Imagine trying to sleep!"

We are on a roll now. A young doctor who carried out her year of compulsory rural service in the small town of Yopál tells me that even there, stuck way out in the plains stretching to Venezuela, with a population of no more than twenty thousand, a cosmic surgeon would fly in and do four liposuctions every weekend, drawing in patients from the surrounding countryside. She also recalls working in the emergency room of a Bogotá hospital, draining liters of pus from each buttock of a woman whose oil implants had gone septic. Liters!

"People fly in from the USA, and Colombia now leads Brazil in this field," my friend Olivia said as she prepared lunch for me in her stifling cinderblock house at the end of town, while I watched what seemed like a documentary but was actually a ten-minute advertisement for a "vibrating corset" that promised to eliminate fat through *electronic massage*. "People have died," she told me, glancing at the TV. "From perforated intestines."

I suppose death from perforated intestines is worse than what I hear of from my musician friend Gloria. Her friend built up her ass with silicone only to have it gradually slide down her legs. I see it sliding as I write. *Lipo* is mad dangerous, she tell me. "Some bodies simply can't take it. Anyway," she continued, "you love a person regardless of their appearance. As you get older, you lose the beauty of youth, but so what!" That's all very well for Gloria. She is a fervent Evangelist. The things of this world, other than her singing and music, don't seem all that important to her, now she has been able to recreate a bond with her husband, thanks to the frenzy of this new passion sweeping through town, a substitute for cosmic surgery.

Close by lives a young nurse who has a job in the organ transplant ward of a fancy clinic in the city of Cali. She is one of the lucky ones. Not only does she have a job, but it's a good job, way beyond the dreams of her neighbors. One day she decided to have her nose altered by a doctor in the clinic. Like quite a few Afro-Colombian women I have met she disliked her *nariz chata*, as it is called. Her aunt told me that a few days before he went on holiday the cosmic surgeon accosted her. "Oh! I have to fix your nose quickly before I leave!" But the operation went badly. Months later she went to another surgeon for a second operation. "Now she breathes like a cat," her aunt told me (meaning she purrs, I suppose). "You know how a cat breathes? You can hear her breathing several feet away. She has constant headaches because she goes in and out of air-conditioned rooms and can't breathe properly."

A year later she had liposuction. She was only twenty-eight years old. And slender. She said she needed it because she wanted to wear her clothes that were now too tight. But after the operation she found she couldn't face putting them on! "It makes me ashamed in front of God," she said, because by then she had become an Evangelist.

Now she spends money wildly, locking her bedroom door in her mother's home and staying up till dawn sorting through semiprecious stones she has bought, along with the bronze ornaments like miniature stirrups that fill every inch of space other than the bed, which is strewn with money. The neighbors hear her through the wall at two in the morning, moving furniture. She has no girlfriend or boyfriend. She has bought a new car, unthinkable for most of the people in this town. And she drives way too fast.

People come from all over the world to the transplant ward in which she works, especially from Israel, looking for a kidney, and somehow manage to get to the front of the queue. A new kidney, a new nose, a thinner body, bigger breasts, a bigger ass, driving way too fast . . .

A strange young woman, that's for sure. But the cosmic surgeon sounds pretty strange too. And how might we talk about these strangenesses? Shall we refer them to standard psychology and pathology, or should we invent a new science?

I am thinking of the cosmic surgeon I met in the city of Pereira, elaborating on the notion that everyone suffers from a gap between the way they see their body and what it "really" looks like. But it seems to me that this is not the only gap. There is also the gap between our appearance and the ideal. Who among us does not see oneself as "off," as incomplete or inadequately endowed? And now—with the advent of cosmic surgery—the gap is made ever larger.

I suppose this is a commonplace observation, yet it is something we don't want to think about too much. It could drive us crazy, as with the nurse-cum-purring cat lady. How do I see myself, anyway? Aren't there many versions of me, according to my mood and the time of day? Who is to say what I "really" look like? Every photograph of me is different. As for feeling the gap between my appearance and "the ideal," the same uncertainties apply. But with the craze for cosmic surgery comes the moment of clarity. Now I am conscious of being less than ideal. Yes, I am lacking! Yes, I carry a stigma! Yes, I will change the way I look! But then, what's this? No sooner have I changed myself than I begin again. Only this time my snub nose has gone and I breathe like a cat.

Today, most everywhere, self-consciousness as to one's appearance is acute. Surely this has been true in many places at many times throughout the history of humankind? But has it ever been as tortured and as cruel as today? Hard on the emotions and harder still on logic. For the whole point of this system is that the gap can never be closed. "Mirror, mirror on the wall. Who is the fairest of them all?"

If I were to try to explain to myself why this tortured dissatisfaction with self—joined to the passions of sex and beauty—is so exquisitely prevalent today, I would resort to the following gobbledygook:

the dissatisfaction is the price we pay for the sexualization of commodities in the reign of reality become virtual. The argument would be that now, as never before (a hazardous claim), it is images that grant the world sparkle and substance and that now, just as image-makers have Photoshop, we have extraordinary surgical means to manipulate the image that is one's self.

Yet I would caution here against a one-sided view of humanity struggling pathetically to conform to some postulated ideal. For maybe the gap between one's self-image and the real has a good deal to do with the wish to play with reality, to play with metamorphoses, to stop being what you are right now and become something else, and then, who knows, become still another something else, and so on? Cosmic surgery does have this potential, as the French performance artist Orlan has in startling ways brought to our attention, as through multiple surgeries she has had to become—not younger or more beautiful—but someone or something else.

Being like a cat is not such a bad thing and maybe even a very good thing. And then she wants to change again. And again. We interpret the story in tragic terms, as a stupid surgical intervention gone wrong, and take note of the labored breathing, which we are told is like that of a cat. What an odd note this provides! The Cheshire cat in *Alice in Wonderland* is nothing but smile, while this cosmically crafted cat is only the noise of its nose, something to be further explored by cosmic surgeons catering to those among us who might wish to breathe like an animal—a camel, perhaps, or a fire-breathing dragon, to ward off threatening young men and obviate the need to hire a temporary bodyguard merely to walk to the town center, which is what other people are now doing.

"He is similar," wrote Roger Caillois in a magnificent essay on mimicry, getting everything right but the gender. "He is similar, not similar to something, but just *similar*. And he invents spaces of which he is the convulsive possession."[2] The cat lady provides us with an instance of just such a space—the bedroom locked late at night, the heaps of jewels and brass, the bed awash with peso notes, the loudly sliding furniture—a space of dreams, of transformation, an invented space of which she is the convulsive possession, breathing hard.

mythological warfare

A BLACK PROTUBERANCE CATCHES THE LIGHT. Something the likes of which I have never seen, posing all manner of riddles as to how this our universe is put together. It moves but slowly, and its ribbed, rubbery surface gives off a black sheen that is assuredly more than plastic.

Up the thigh it stretches. But my eyes don't dare go there.

All I get is the fragment as I hurry along the sidewalk on my way to the Universidad Nacional, notorious for its uppity students wearing masks and hurling Molotov cocktails at the police when the latter dare enter the sacred bubble that is the campus, emblazoned with a giant portrait of Che. It is wonderful in the bubble. Like being in a different country, with its own border controls and curious customs. Most of the boys wear their beautiful long black hair like Kogi Indians, way past their shoulders, and are hard to distinguish from the girls. All is calm today. The sun shines benignly now and again between crazy thunderstorms that hurl themselves out of nowhere from the other side of Monserate and Guadalupe, the dark mountains that loom above Bogotá with white crucifixes on their peaks, as if, like the body of the Savior, they have been nailed to a turbulent sky, a sky like those El Greco was wont to paint behind his crucifixions. The baroque, again. It is of comfort, is it not, that mountains too have names like Monserate and Guadelupe? Then I realize this thing that is like no other thing is a knee, but like no other knee. It is a knee encased in armor.

Another quick sideways glance as I gain confidence. It is a man in armor. A man like no other man. Did I see right?

Funny how fast the mind works at such times, like what happens when you are drowning, perhaps. The kneecaps, I figure, are so he can drop to the ground and open fire nice and steady with his automatic weapon. But does he *really* need this? Do the US soldiers in Afghanistan *really* need this? It certainly makes walking difficult and clumsy, but then those soldiers mostly ride in armored vehicles, don't they?

So maybe there is some other need at work here, like the need for the grotesque, and the curdling of the ugly. Thinking in terms of efficiency is mere rationalization—what's really in play is the need for weapons of mythogical warfare (as J. M. Coetzee described so well in "The Vietnam Project").[1] Yes! The first need here is to scare people such that the soldiers

- scare *themselves*
- become *supernatural*
- create *theater* and *spectacle*
- *change the face of reality* (William Burroughs: "create a black hole in the fabric of reality, through which the inhabitants of these ancient cities travelled in time to a final impasse."[2])

Another quick sideways glance. This time up the thigh. Another fragment. I spy a huge *codpiece* made of the same rubbery, ribbed black shiny stuff. It is bulging, as if it held the genitals of a horse or that lover of Jean Genet in *The Thief's Journal*, the one packing grapes in his crotch.

I am transported to the Middle Ages. A codpiece! The critical area where my power resides, which my enemy wants. The codpiece, not the spurs, is "the first piece of harness in the arming of a warrior," says Panurge in Rabelais's *Gargantua*. Its job is to protect a man's bollocks, Panurge explains, drawing on the biblical authority of the fig leaf and noting its "curliness, smoothness, size, colour, smell, virtues, and faculties for arming and covering," although, he points out, there will always be those mighty bollocks that cannot be easily accommodated, like those of the noble Valentine, who used to spread his out on a table like a Spanish cloak so he could scrub them clean.[3]

But does not the mighty bulge of my codpiece draw attention to my vulnerability and even, perhaps, draw my enemy's ire and fire? Is it not all the more atttacting in its repulsing?

Perhaps the Bogotá fashion house of Miguel Caballero, specializing in bulletproof apparel, knows the answer? Called the Armani of bulletproof clothing, its website claims to have "created a fresh line of Italian themed clothing featuring blazers, leather jackets, coats, rain-coats, dress shirts, t-shirts, polos, vests and more. All of them are lightweight and easy to wear." They provide protection against "sub machine guns such as mini Uzis and even high powered assault rifles and machine guns like the MP5."[4]

This is the beauty of the knight in black armor I came across outside the university, the new riot police, more ornately known by the acronym ESMAD—which, pronounced in Spanish, comes across as *is mad*, which pretty well gets it right. Meanwhile, the full title—Escuadron Movil Anti-Disturbios—has that nice, pompous, lethargic horror that seems indispensable to authority.

Videos show these ESMAD guys proudly displaying their uniforms, the camera pausing tenderly on the flamboyant codpieces, even more than on their hefty, Humvee-like water cannons. Other videos, shot by students in Cali during pitched street battles, reveal how tortoiselike and cumbersome these water cannons are. The ESMAD guys are equally clumsy, while masked students dart hither and thither with elegant ease, hurling Molotov cocktails that, on concussion, pour orange and yellow flame onto the water cannons. It is a spectacular performance, a ballet of death, and both sides seem to enjoy it.

Protesters in Cairo's Tahrir Square in 2011 went further. Photographs show them, facing camouflage-painted tanks and tough-looking soldiers, clad in their own version of "riot gear." One angry young man has swaths of transparent plastic wrapped around his head, holding a slim loaf of bread vertically by his right ear, as if it were an antenna or something unimaginably sinister. Another, more meditative fellow with a mustache has placed a kitchen pot over his head, held in place by a red cloth. Still another has somehow affixed a garbage can lid to his head, looking for all the world like a

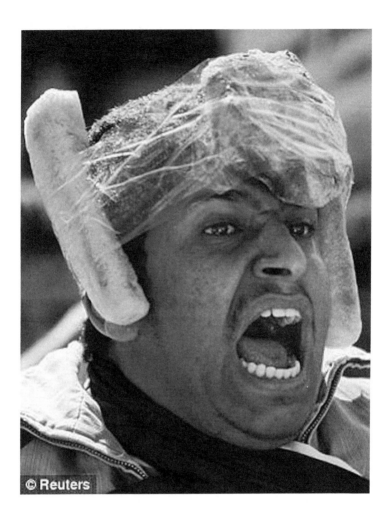

© Reuters

Vietnamese peasant in a rice field. The effect is gorgeous, and suddenly the sinister melodrama of the state's mythological warfare has been punctured. Through this mix of humor and protest aesthetics as prosthetics, the sublime has been laughed away, just like the doggerel of Occupy Wall Street protestors celebrating two months of occupation on November 17, 2011, in Portland, Oregon, when confronted by police in riot gear:

> You're sexy, you're cute
> Take off your riot suit![5]

Photo by Yannick Tylle, European Pressphoto Agency.

The Bogotá riot gear I saw now exists the world over, a return to the aesthetic of the Middle Ages or the baroque splendor beloved by Don Quixote, except the knights in armor fighting for a woman's honor are now thugs working for the modern state, everywhere but everywhere geared up to crush a supposed surge of "anarchists," also dressed in black.

The outstanding design feature of riot police aesthetics at the G20 meeting in Toronto in June 2010 was the terrible, crashing, rhythmic sound. It was like all the devils had erupted from the earth. As presented in numerous videos on YouTube, the police advanced in rows occupying the width of the street, beating in unison on their body-length, transparent shields, with P-O-L-I-C-E written diagonally across in big black letters. The sound is hypnotic. It mimics their heavy tread as well as the frightened pulse beating in your ears, now merged into one doomsday rhythm. Like chaff in the wind your body is taken over by the *blitzkrieg*, here in the gentle land of the maple leaf, a strikingly choreographed instance of designer terrorism, now the new normal. News reports never fail to mention the dreaded anarchists dressed in black on such occasions, but rarely, if ever, is the carefully contrived theater of violence enacted by the police a cause for comment or analysis. Some of the police carry weapons that look like antique muskets with trumpet-shaped mouths. Others have bouquets of bright yellow plastic handcuffs jiggling from their knees. With the masks of their helmets down, over the face, they shut down the world—the normal world, that is. Others, with their masks up, protruding, at right angles to their faces, appear like so many giant cockroaches, devouring everything in their path.[6]

I ask myself about the design choices that shape this creature, this man in his riot gear, not to mention his flashing lights, his sirens and other "sonic weapons," his tear gas, his tanks, and his horse. Is this not of a piece with cosmic surgery? Or rather, is this not the flip side—the dark side—of cosmic surgery, akin to the stories people love to tell of cosmic surgery gone wrong?

What, then, is this cosmic surgery–enhanced body encased in armor? What does it tell us about the new body set forth in the world today? And what is its relation to storytelling?

Let me answer by recalling again the 1937 essay in which Walter Benjamin suggests that the art of storytelling is coming to an end and that this has a complicated connection to death or, rather, to the type of death we associate with modernity, whether on the battlefield or in the intensive care unit, stuffed with tubes, far from home. It is a complicated relation because death can also be that which sustains the art of storytelling, as his essay amply illustrates, with reference to what we might call "premodern death." Hence, I would like to suggest that instead of coming to an end, as Benjamin says, a new type of story emerges or is enhanced, the story that circles the new body that is also the body of the world.

Benjamin gives us a picture, a picture of German soldiers returning from the front at the end of World War I unable to talk about their experience—because they had none, or rather because their long-term experience had been displaced by rapid-fire, fragmentary, instantaneous lived moments that are expunged from memory as soon as they are "experienced." In lieu of experience, Benjamin gives us a body, a forlorn and isolated body, naked to the winds of history, like Lear on the heath.

Noteworthy in Benjamin's formulation is the playoff between the human body and experience, as if the more damaging the impact on our capacity to experience, the more important the body becomes, until there exists only the body. But then you have to ask, What sort of body is this?

It is a body, Benjamin famously says, that stands "under the open sky in a countryside in which nothing remained unchanged but the clouds, and beneath those clouds, in a field of force of destructive torrents and explosions, was the tiny fragile human body."[7]

It is a body, thus, that stands in for experience, a body all body—and here's my point—like that body now targeted by cosmic surgery in the force field of a peasant economy wracked by war and agribusiness, "in which nothing remains unchanged but the clouds"—only now even the clouds are changing as planet earth reacts to industrial poisoning. It is in this situation that stories about the horrors of cosmic surgery abound. Yet on Benjamin's reckoning storytelling has ended or is coming to an end.

So we have to make some adjustments, because what we have here are new and different types of stories, geared to a space between life and death, a state of emergency that, given today's world, is not the exception but the rule. These are stories bound to penultimateness—the *moment that is permanently the moment before the last*. There is no last. No end. Or rather, it is all end all the time. This introduces a novel sense of time, the continuous ending, which seems to me appropriate to a world given over to a continuous sense of catastrophe, in which "the black hole in the fabric of reality" is every day amplified.

How fascinating that this type of story—the story that continually ends stories—should be so intimately bound up with the fate of the human body subject to beautification. This could only occur, I feel, or come into its fullest expression, in a country where cosmetic surgery—*cosmic surgery*—exists as an art that includes mutilation, creating an intertwined aesthetic practice of beauty and the beast.

beauty and mutilation

MUTILATION OF THE BODY, DEAD OR ALIVE, has a history in Colombia stretching back at least to the *violencia clasica* of the late 1940s and 1950s, when it was by no means uncommon for the members of opposing political parties—Liberals and Conservatives—to artfully work each other over with machete and knife. The mutilations were given designer names: the *corte de corbata*, or necktie cut, in which the flesh under the jaw is cut open and the tongue pulled through; the *corte de franela*, in which the muscles holding the head are cut, such that it flops back perpendicular to the spine; the *bocachico*, in which shallow slits are made in the living body and the victim slowly bleeds to death (the name refers to a common form of preparing fish for frying, making parallel slits along both sides); the *corte de florero*, or flower vase cut; *the corte de mico*, or monkey cut; the *corte frances*, or French cut; and so forth. These were supplemented with rape, genital mutilation, and extracting the living fetus from the womb and killing it.[1]

Thirty years later this aesthetic of creative mutilation resurfaced in the surgeries practiced by Colombian paramilitary groups, some of which reportedly ran mutilation schools that, at the same time, served as initiation. One paramilitary, Francisco Villaba, alias Christian Barreto, described attending such a school in the 1990s, at which students were made to dismember living persons to obtain information.[2]

"Not even prayer can relieve me of the fear I felt then," a young woman paramilitary told the Colombian writer Alfredo Molano. "They tied him up on the ground and beat him till he was like a bag of bones, cut his legs off at the knee with a machete while he still alive, then the arms, asking 'Does that hurt? Does that hurt? You fuck!' And then the face; the nose, the lips, the ears. Just a lump of living flesh was what was left." The guerrilla had their tricks too, she hastens to add.[3]

Cosmic surgery is the signature act of the *paras*, whose strategy— if we can use such a highfalutin word for so elementary an act—is to send an unmistakable message, as through mutilation with their favored instrument, the power saw. The designer smile given to the paramilitary chieftain Salvatore Mancuso is this butchery's perverse complement, as in one of those horror movies where smiling faces and mutilated bodies go together, beauty and the beast, the chuckling villain and his despoiled victims. Too like a kid's cartoon, *Tom and Jerry* or *Bugs Bunny,* this image is too, too terribly real. The more he carves them up, the more he gets his fancy dentist to sharpen his smile, not to mention his teeth.

In the early 1980s in the small frontier town of Mocoa where the Andes tumble into the Amazon basin, I saw a large, window-filling, advertisement for a Stihl chain saw. A sit-foot-high cardboard cut-out, it showed a young blonde woman in short pants seated on the ground with her back pressed up against a dark tree trunk. Between her outstretched legs lay a power saw aimed at her crotch.

Ten years later I heard of the paramilitary massacre in the town of Trujillo in the Cauca Valley. Several hundred people had been tortured and killed, some—maybe most—dismembered by power saws, including the Jesuit priest Father Tiberio Fernández who was said to have been castrated and decapitated. He could well have been alive when they started.

The arts of bodily mutilation do not stop there, however. Frequently one hears of the face obliterated by acid, the eyes sewn shut, and the fingers amputated. And as if that's not enough, it is said that the bodies are thrown into the river, sometimes with stones in the abdominal cavity so the bodies sink. When asked, people with whom I speak, shrug and say they don't really understand why this is done. Others come forward with practical reasons—or what they claim to be practical reasons—to do with concealing the identity of the victim, but I think all this is essentially a ritual of obliteration of the body made all the more magical by dressing it up as "practical."

As a form of cosmic surgery, bodily mutilation has its own aesthetic ensuring that memory will be everlasting, as Nietzsche tells us in *The Genealogy of Morality*. "When man decided he had to make a memory," he writes, "it never happened without blood, torments and sacrifices (the sacrifice of the first born belongs here), the most disgusting mutilations (for example, castration) . . . all this has its origin in that particular instinct which discovered that pain is the most powerful aid to mnemonics." In Nietzsche's estimation, cruelty not only continues in a curiously "deified" form today but, he says, is actually constitutive of modern culture. "To see somebody suffer is nice," he writes. "To make somebody suffer even nicer."[4]

With images of US army guards in Abu Ghraib in mind, not to mention what we hear from Guantanamo Bay, we have to credit Nietzsche's insights here, most especially as regards the theatrical (read "festival") dimensions inseparable from torture.

Nietzsche might seem to be saying that the aesthetic of cruelty was something that existed way back in the past and that what we see today is something that occurs only in "backward" corners of the world—such as Colombian paramilitaries and the states of Texas and Georgia, notorious for their execution mania—as well as in the "war machine" of modern states, meaning the police and army. In addition, he could be interpreted along Freudian lines as saying that the "civilizing process" involves repression of instincts such that when cruelty emerges it does so with considerable force, like a volcano erupting, and lacks that "innocence" of ancient times and the festival to which he alludes. But Nietzsche offers a more complex and more compelling picture when he argues that this civilizing process (what he calls *ressentiment*) actually requires and depends upon violence and cruelty as part of its inner life and does so in a specially aestheticized manner involving elaborate mimicry such as we find in certain styles of theater—as when he remarks that the criminal today becomes hardened because he sees his actions mimicked by the forces of law *in the name of justice—*

and given approval, practiced with good conscience: like spying, duping, bribing, setting traps, the whole intricate and wily skills of the policeman and prosecutor, as well as the most thorough robbery, violence, slander, imprisonment, torture and murder, carried out without even having emotion as an excuse.[5]

In the name of justice. That's the rub. Yet if mimicry like this is diabolically nasty—finding justification "in the name of justice," as does paramilitary cosmic surgery—how much more theatrical is the ultimate flourish, when the magic of obliteration is set in motion and cosmic surgery reaches is climax thanks to power saws and rivers? But enough! Enough of this melodrama actualized by hoary chaps wielding their tools of trade, lest we perfect their very machination. Let us take stock of the mundane everyday and slide from the sacred to the profane. Come take a walk to the street corner where, since many a decade, this same minute attention to the spectacle of violation has existed in another register; namely the presentation of lurid photographs of violated corpses and of nude or almost nude young women, side by side in daily newspaers such as *El Caleno*, *El Espacio*, and *El Bogotano.* Vendors display full-page spreads to attract customers, but also as a public service, if one is to judge by the appreciative, mainly male, crowd that gathers to absorb this daily serving of sex and mutilation, here more than reconciled, thanks to the everydayness of the newspaper lying face up on the cold pavement.

It is so easy to be frightened by designer terror, first, because it is terrifying and, second, because it becomes even more so when you realize that it is designed and not simply the outpouring of rage, bullying, and frustration. To come across designer terror lite, as in the newspaper laid out on the pavement, is to breathe a little easier, I think, because you can get a grip on the real horrors that lie beyond. It is like vaccination.

But how much more is this the case with the inspired counter-aesthetic of the young man in Tahrir Square with his head swathed in ClingWrap, thereby supporting a loaf of bread as an antenna? So much for the media hype about the importance of Twitter and digital media, he is saying. This is real bread on a real head and a really unreal symbolic antenna. So much for the bogeymen of the state's repressive apparatus. Yes, of course they are scary. I recall seeing the monsters let loose on the streets of Paris in May '68, giants with their medieval shields, clad from chin to shin in black leather coats, beasts of prey hidden away in caves and cages being thrown red meat every day until let loose when the state was cornered. But that was also a struggle in which wit and beauty took to the streets as oppositional force and as something more than opposition, namely a cry for a new world, a messianic movement, like Occupy Wall Street forty years later. Through art locked into designer terror, the body with its ClingWrap uniform steps smartly into history and revolution, resuming the dance between the art of terror and that which terror fears most, the art of humor. Such ClingWrap art takes advantage of the way that terror, and especially designer terror, is but a hairbreadth from kids' cartoons that substitute animals such as mice and bunny rabbits for people. Along with Rabelais, it takes the sting out of those silly codpieces and grown men beating on shields. The extraction of the comic element in those striving for power, their reliance on the mute absurd, turns fear into laughter and protest into carnival. The great cartoonist Chuck Jones may have thought it easier to humanize animals than to humanize humans, but ClingWrap artists the world over go one better, humanizing us all, animals included, not though demythologizing mythological warfare but through its reenchantment.

the exploding breast

"COLOMBIA IS A COUNTRY OF *PARAS* AND *NARCOS*," the surgeon tells me straight up as I settle into my chair in a palatial cosmic surgery clinic in Pereira, a city where the mountains loom and the wealth, once from hogs, coffee, and textiles, now comes from cocaine, cosmic surgery, and the fashion industry. I hear stories of luxurious homes nearby, such as the house with floors of crystal with fish swimming underneath.

It is shocking to be told from the get-go that this is a land of *paras* and *narcos*. This is the orienting posture, your GPS. "In the beginning was the word . . ." You begin at that point, and you end up with another form of cosmogenesis in the form of cosmic surgery.

"You know Cartago?" the nutritionist asks me. "It's only a few miles away. Imagine. It is late afternoon like now, still warm outside, and the *narcos* and the *paras* will be sitting there by the sidewalk drinking beer and eying the girls who parade past. A market of female flesh. Poor girls from twelve to twenty years of age. And their mothers? They are selling their daughters. All these girls want surgery."

"All those narcos care about is how big your breasts are, says a Colombian TV actress. If they want you, the first thing they do is send you to their plastic surgeons to have silicone implants. But it's them who decide how big you should be, not you."[1] Actually, the first thing they sent early one morning was a new BMW wrapped in

MI BUSTO POR UN REINO

De las 23 candidatas del próximo concurso de belleza, 19 se hicieron cirugía del busto, con el propósito de tener más argumentos para conquistar la corona. Para los sicólogos, el asunto tiene que ver con la autoestima. Los medios de comunicación, dicen los expertos, difunden unos arquetipos de belleza para seguir. Hay defensores y detractores de esta moda de fin de siglo.

MÁS INFORMACIÓN PÁGINAS 4-C y 5-C

*My bust for a kingdom.*Front page of *El Espectador,* one of Colombia's most esteemed newspapers, Ocober 9, 1998. Photo by Juan Carlos Guerrero Beltran.

a pink ribbon and parked in the driveway. And sometimes they get to decide a lot more than the size of your bosom, like maybe killing you as well, which is what my neighbor told me about the beautiful daughter of the local postmaster who married a narco and a year later was found murdered.

"Beautiful girls want to partner up with *narcos* on account of their money," my neighbor told me, shaking her head. "Beautiful girls exploit their beauty. They don't want to study. What they want is to live in great luxury, *en buen lujo—por eso hay tanto interes en cirujía plastica!* That's why there's so much interest in plastic surgery."

Once upon a time not so long ago women around here made their own clothes in their own homes, thanks to Singer sewing machines and to immigrants from the Middle East who walked the back roads with cloth to sell. Once upon a time women wore skirts and revealed little of their bodies. Once upon a time fashion was a sedate affair, a long-held plateau of sameness without, so it seems to me, much interest beyond being neat and clean and if possible having a pair of shoes. That's what I encountered in 1970, when most people still had farms, small as they were. But today that seems like a prehistoric time, and fashion has become a thing, a great grand thing, like a meteor crashing through the black sky. It is the young, especially the young, who carry this new history on their bodies, as if, now landless, all the minutiae of care once bestowed on their intricate farms of trees, has been transferred to the care of the appearance of the body. And just as the plantations on all sides of the life-world technologize the land with chemicals for this and that, newer and bigger machinery for this and that, massive tractor trailers rumbling through country lanes stirring up mighty clouds of dust, so the body of the young people, bereft of land, becomes increasingly technologized as well. The body changes in a fundamental way. The body that is ours, no less than the body of the world that was once ours, is now theirs, but by rights belongs to all and none.

In that time of "once upon a time"—think of García Márquez's *One Hundred Years of Solitude*—there was no marijuana, just magical realism. Coca existed as coca leaf, not cocaine, and was used only by Indians living in remote places, where it was chewed with lime. Then, for reasons that are as cliched as they are obscure, everything turned upside down. Magical realism became real—or entirely magical, depending on how you look at things. In the 1980s cocaine production kicked in, for export and later for widespread domestic use; the guerrilla war took off, followed by the paramiliatry counterguerrilla offensive and an increase in US military intervention. And fashion become an ever bigger business, teaming up internationally with the art world as the new Medicis—Goldman Sachs, Lehmann Brothers, and their ilk—started to invest in art.

By the late 1990s female beauty, of the body and its trappings, had become not only an industry but the glowing tip of the fiery messenger announcing that we had moved on from once-upon-a-time snail-time to meteor-time destined for a brilliant conflagration of continuous *depense*, notably the narco breast with its uncanny stories. One such story concerns the security operation that makes sure you don't fly away after surgery until your breasts have been in place a week, lest they explode in midair due to changes in pressure.

"I was in the plane sitting next to a prostitute on her way back to Spain," my friend's mother told me. "Just before we took off from Pereira the stewardess came up and told her she had to deplane as the surgery was too fresh. She couldn't stop sobbing, saying she had to be back in Spain in two days or she would lose her job. You know, women have died from their breasts exploding in midair after surgery."

But the handsome young cosmic surgeon assured me otherwise. With that smoothly shaved confidence with which surgeons are blessed, as if from birth, he informed me that the exploding breast was a myth. "The breasts we install have a 100 percent change potential," he said. Yet a year later the Colombian media was full of the terrible story of a beautiful TV news anchor and lingerie model, Laura Acuña, whose left breast had indeed "exploded," or at least leaked, causing her intense pain.

The surgeon also claimed that he was 200 percent busy. Not surprising given that by the time they are pushing forty, many women fear their husbands will take up with some svelte young thing. Yet does it do any good? In Santa Marta, María told me of a friend who, after her husband left her for a younger, prettier woman, had her breasts and buttocks enlarged, only to be told by her son, "*Mami*, what he wants is a woman of twenty, not a woman who seems twenty."

Downtown in a less exclusive clinic in drab office building on a busy street, another cosmic surgeon with an endearing, football-shaped face, wearing blue jeans, took me slowly through a slide show on his computer. He had done his training in Brazil, where the emphasis, he explained, lay on breast reduction and ass enlargement. He had never been asked to perform a breast reduction in Colombia.

First he laid out three or four breasts—breast implants, that is—in front of the computer. They are similar, he said, to the implants used for the buttocks and for the calves. There they lay like so many jellyfish—pale translucent orbs of varying sizes. I was surprised by their weight, let alone that I had the temerity to pick them up. The 350 cc breast weighs a full pound, he told me, and is the most commonly used in Colombia (compared with 80 cc in Brazil). Imagine having to carry two of those all the time. Here I was, a man learning the basic facts of life.

He was a great teacher. Switching on his computer, he presented a slide show of his recent work. Flashing across the screen were bloody pictures of surgery and immediate post-op situations. Most of the images were faceless, showing just breasts. Now and again there was a photograph of a woman's face in bitter distress. A fleeting image, but that was enough. Reality became extra real sitting in the dark-paneled doctor's office watching this parade of body parts, so at odds with the dream of beauty and the perfect body these procedures strive to produce. This was hard work for all concerned. Phrases like "nip and tuck," while appreciated for their levity, exist precisely because this stuff is serious.

"*400 Tetas En Peligro*" (400 Breasts in Danger), read one image on his screen taken from a local newspaper. The women in question had sought out backyard cosmic surgeons who injected their breasts with cooking oil so as to enlarge them. A photograph showed a hideously deformed young woman who ended up having a double mastectomy.

Strange things happened in this room, apparently. And I am not surprised. For there was not that much difference between it and what I imagine a medieval alchemist's chamber was like, where base metals were turned into gold. There was the young woman with a scar on her chest who would come every day for a consultation and ask the surgeon to fuck her. Later he learned she was the girlfriend of a *narco*. There was the woman who wanted him to operate on her husband's face. He had died that morning. I wondered why he was telling me this, his face bashful and incredulous in turns.

Discussing the place of allegory in the baroque, Benjamin refers us to the importance of fragmentation, as in "the untidy and disordered character of magicians' dens or alchemists' laboratories familiar, above all, to the baroque."[2] This, he insists, is of a piece with seeing nature as poetic—and I have to ask myself what could be more poetic and more thematized as "fragmentary" than these artificial breasts laid out on the dark desk of this cosmic surgeon, alchemist of the body?

Stranger still is that the self-titled "most Colombian of all Colombian artists," Fernando Botero, comes from Medellin, located in the same region as Pereira, and for decades he has obsessively painted pictures of fat people, nothing but white fatties except for a few fat horses. Was this in anticipatory defiance of the cult of thinnness that would burst upon the scene in the 1990s? Was it an omen of the epidemic of obesity and liposuction that would occur around the same time, even in this poor country? Botero is the artist of the rotund. He makes a virtue of the grotesque. He makes fatness charming, a bitter-sweet parody of conventions now held dear. I notice that while copies of his work hang on my dentist's walls in Manhattan ("great Third World art"), they are not to be found on the walls of the cosmic surgeons I visit in Colombia. I myself think of his fat people, with their beady unblinking eyes and porcine faces, as the fabled rich peasants of central Colombia in an earlier epoch, rich with pigs and coffee farms, prizing girth and large families with ten or even twenty children. They are the *kulaks* you see depicted with tender distaste by the Soviet filmmaker Sergei Eisenstein in his 1929 film *The Old and The New*, double chins dribbling down onto fat hairy chests or ample bosoms with jewel necklaces, while the rest of the villagers starve. They are the hefty chiefs and bloated oil-billionaire dictator-presidents of Africa, where fat means power and prestige. How fitting that in Colombia, at least, the great art of fatties and the great arts of cosmic surgery occur side by side.

Some say history proceeds not through gradual evolution but through big shifts in blinks of the eye. That's certainly how the history of the birth of cosmic surgery came across to me in Pereira— which I take as a microcosm of both the nation and the notion of beautification of women, Pereira being legendary for its mix of splendid cosmic surgery and splendid prostitutes. As for the fame of its prostitutes, how can one explain such a thing? My guide tells me that its reputation came about in the mid-nineteenth century, when the town was a privileged "truck stop," so to speak, for mule trains. This is where the north-south and east-west trails intersected. Sex and commerce. So what else is new? Same for the bankers on Wall Street as for the hoary truck drivers pulling over in Kalamazoo,

Michigan. But this sort of fact is hardly granted the importance it deserves in studies of the economic development of this or any other country.

The story I was told many times over when I asked why Pereira was such a beacon for cosmic surgery had to do with an earthquake. Everyone agreed. It was the terrible trauma of the earthquake in 1999 that ushered in this bonanza—because the earthquake was followed by massive aid from Spain, which included the offer of visas, an offer eagerly taken up by the city's renowned prostitutes, who found the working conditions in Spain superior and soon used their euros to travel home to take advantage of cheaper and high-quality cosmic surgery to stay comely.

History may indeed proceed through cataclysmic shifts—an earthquake or an exploding breast—but it needs to elaborate images to do so. In this regard, stories of extremity and disaster seem as necessary as the other sort of fairy tale that uses disaster as an anvil on which to beat out a message of hope, which springs eternal in the human breast.

virtual u

DEEP IN THE ARCHIVE THAT HOLDS a lock of the hair of the Liberator, Simón Bolívar, I bumped into an old friend who teaches at the local university, which, so they say, is the oldest in the Americas. He too is old, now, and has been here too long, disappointed too many times, nursing his grievances with the cold comfort of parody. Why! he tells me, with a grand gesture meant to hide a bitter grimace, *es una universidad virtual*—it's a virtual University!

Nothing but a web page, he says. A magnificent web page full of images of the president of the university and the ever more numerous vice presidents, shown on their their recent trips to China. The word *magnifica* rolls slowly off his lips to fall into his outstretched hands, a golden bauble turning to offal in the fetid air. On *magnificent* per diems, he adds, over an animated lunch in a dark restaurant off a side street where we huddle like conspirators stabbing reality with our forks. As for the professors, well, they don't teach any more. They become research professors—he rolls his eyes—padding their salaries by sucking up to NGOs, which are kept busy doing good in a country like Colombia, as you can well imagine. What little teaching takes place is carried out by underpaid and uncaring adjuncts. To cap it off, the students don't attend classes but nevertheless graduate. Everyone is happy in Virtual U.

He asks me what I am doing, and I tell him I am researching the history of beauty and cosmic surgery. Have you seen the woman in the archive? his consort asks me, giggling like a teenager, as if disclosing a secret that is not all that secret. Sure enough, in the dim light of the archive, its walls lined top to bottom with leather-bound volumes, there is a young woman whose figure speaks eloquently of surgical intervention. This is accompanied by heavy facial makeup and a flirtatious manner, despite the gravity of her posture, seated in the panoptic position overlooking the scholars, who in turn are bent over their yellowing papers.

As is now well known, thanks to the labors of Michel Foucault, the panopticon, as conceptualized by Jeremy Bentham in the late eighteenth century, is structured like a cartwheel with a hub from which radiate spokes, allowing a person at the center to see everyone at the periphery. The people at the periphery cannot tell whether they are being watched, nor can they see their similarly situated fellows. Prime examples are the so-called model prison and the old reading room of the British Museum, where Karl Marx, and lesser folk like me, labored as if in solitary confinement, with only the ever-watchful spirit of the Enlightenment to keep us company. It is a powerful image and one more relevant today than in the eighteenth century, for ours is truly the age of the surveillance state and the "Patriot Act."

Yet in the archive containing Simon Bolívar's lock of hair, the panoptic relation seems reversed, for the person at the center, who is supposed to see without being seen, is in fact displaying herself. She is there to be seen—and not seen—and this, surely, is how power works too, with the king's two bodies, one visible, the other hidden, like George W. Bush and his sidekick, Dick Cheney, hidden in his "secure, undisclosed location," except for his snarl, posing as a smile.

I recall the soldiers of the Colombian army patrolling the streets of one of the more notorious cocaine-producing towns, La Hormiga, in the Putumayo, in 2006. It was decidedly unreal. Everyone in the street—people sitting at the tables of cheaper-than-cheap cafes, the moving mass of pedestrians, riders of motorbikes, vendors in stalls selling knickknacks and showing DVDs of seminaked ladies dancing—everyone seemed to be watching the soldiers while at the same time appearing to be oblivious of them. In fact, it would be dangerous to look the soldiers in the eye or display much awareness as to their presence. They are there, and they are not there. But a small dog saves the day. Wagging its tail, it walks along with the soldiers, best of friends. Reared in jungle towns, this little dog pauses to raise its hind leg and pee on a light pole. Now when I think of what it takes to look and not look simultaneously, to be seen and not seen simultaneously, I think back to this happy little dog trotting along, as if the animal—only the animal—can embody this complicated optical maneuver, at once sophisticated and intuitive.

There are other bodies to conjure with here along with the animal, such as the bodies strolling through the mall emitting contradictory signals. You would need the wit and insight of Charles Baudelaire to express its complexities, as with his mid-nineteenth-century description of the *flaneur* as a kaleidescope with consciousness. The flaneur enters into the crowd, wrote Baudelaire, as though it were an immense reservoir of electrical energy. Above all it is fashion, meaning changes in dress and deportment, that captures the flaneur's eye—his eagle eye—but, in his hurrying and searching, this solitary fellow (who reminds me of myself and of anthropological fieldwork) is possessed by an even loftier aim, for he "makes it his business to extract from fashion whatever element it may contain of poetry within history."[1]

Hence the question I want to ask here is what part does *display*—as in the Cali airport or in the archive—what part does such display occupy in Baudelaire's *poetry within history* brought forth by fashion? More pointedly, what part does the *scotoma* play—those arts of revelation and concealment of the female body, of seeing but not being seen seeing, as well as seeing but not seeing what you are seeing?

This is where Baudelaire's flaneur fails us. For there never was nor ever could be such a prince of invisibility. He is ever so much a philosophical conceit and a childhood fantasy of seeing without being seen, a fantasy fortified by the anonymity of the crowds of the modern city. Yet at least Baudelaire's flaneur is enjoying himself and enjoying the crowd as the scene of a thousand and one delights, not like the grim picture presented, for example, by Friedrich Engels in *The Condition of the Working Class in England,* published in 1845 when Engels was but twenty-five years of age. He thought the crowded streets were anathema to human nature. People rushed past each other absorbed in self-interest, typifying the dog-eat-dog world of capitalist competition.[2]

"Hell is a city much like London," wrote the poet Shelley around the same time as Engels, but in this hell we are no longer dealing with mindless ants rushing past each other. Not at all. Suddenly women enter into the picture, and it is the role of such women in Shelley's rendering to make us see something important in the crowd:

Things whose trade is, over ladies
  To lean, and flirt, and stare, and simper,
Till all that is divine in woman
  Grows cruel, courteous, smooth, inhuman,
  Crucified 'twixt a smile and whimper[3]

To bring sex into the fray is to engage with that "immense reservoir of electrical energy" that is Baudelaire's crowd. Nevertheless Baudelaire's sketch of the flaneur is but one half of the picture, the half that concerns the observer. For to look is only half the story. The other half is the look on the face and the movement of the body of the person aware of being looked at.

The truth is that the people the flaneur espies are aware—extremely aware—of being looked at. It is a game. For not only are the observed aware of being observed, but with the dispensation in female fashion of revelation and concealment, their awareness of being observed has moved from a passive into an active realm of display that takes advantage of the observer's conceit that he, like the fabled flaneur, is seeing without being seen seeing.

Scotoma indeed! laughed my friend. Such an *interesting* word! But where does that put your wish to write a history of beauty? What sort of history can be built on seeing as not seeing as the basis of knowing beauty? He paused and in a somewhat mocking tone asked, Is that your kaleidscope with consciousness?

It was as if he could read my thoughts and wanted to play with the scotoma. The person being looked at but not being looked at, he said with painful deliberation, pretends to be not looked at and puts on a *wooden face*. Think about it! he exclaimed, carried away by his image. Wooden faces are now the rage as these exaggerated breasts pop up all over Colombia, like tulips in Holland! One part of the body stands out; another, the face, withdraws into a mask of stolidity. Not only does the person being looked at adopt a wooden face, but the person looking does as well. Her face is saying that she doesn't see you not looking at her. It reminds me, he said, of a game of peek-a-boo like adults play with children, hiding their face behind their hands only to expose it at the last minute, like Virtual U.

Time is running out. I hurry to the terminal to catch a bus out of town. It is dangerous to travel these parts at night. People are milling around the ticket counter. The *ayudantes* yell and drag confused travelers this way and that, with conflicting promises as to which bus will leave first. In this immense reservoir of electrical energy a young woman stands by the door of my bus, as if about to get on. But stock-still. She seems to be waiting for someone. Her gaze is vacant. Her face is wooden. With her blouse worn so low so as to reveal the areola of one breast, she doesn't see the seeing in the midst of the collective, scotomized reality. At the last minute she gets into the bus. Alone. Was she waiting for someone? Or just waiting?

the history of beauty

He has an aim loftier than that of a mere flaneur . . . he makes it his business to extract from fashion whatever element it may contain of poetry within history.

BAUDELAIRE, "The Painter of Modern Life,"[1]

DESTAPE IS HOW THE OLDER GENERATION refers to the today's explosion in dress, or should I say undress. *El destape!* They spit it out and roll their eyes and hold their hands in the air as if to say, What can I do with my daughters?

They might just as well exclaim, *Depense!* Another roll of the eyes. *El depense!*

"Uncovering" is what it means. When censorship in Spain was suddenly relaxed in 1975 with the end of the Franco dictatorship, a mighty barrier fell, like the Berlin Wall, and the subsequent display of female nudity in Spanish films and magazines was termed *el destape.* It has an apocalyptic ring. "Move over," it announces, for the world is now in another orbit. Spain emerged from the shadows and *destape* gestured toward a new way of life, which was not, however, restricted to Spain but spread worldwide. When it began in my town in Colombia in the 1990s, it was like an explosion smashing overnight the shackles of the past. Bound to a ramified sexualization of everyday life—tighter than tight jeans and revealing tops, pronounced camel-toe crotch and bared belly buttons, gang warfare, motorbike magic, constant insecurity and constant murder—it is not hard to see *el destape* as as the mother of all metaphors turned real, thanks to those wayward daughters of time.

Like *depense, destape* shares an affinity with what that preeminently post-'68 philosopher, Jean-Francois Lyotard, called "drift," affecting young people in "all civilizations on a worldwide scale."[2] This was at once a philosophy and a profound shift in the way an epoch came to define itself, not so much in words as in attitude. Lyotard singled out what he called "affective intensity," which, alongside eroticization ("decoupling of libidinal force") and a fascination, if not obsession, with the aesthetics of everyday life, implied a totally new attitude toward work, to exchange, and—I know of no other way to put this—to the "way things go together," what at one point Lyotard calls "necessity," as in, a "successful attack on the belief in necessity would inevitably lead to the destruction of kapital's main-spring, the alleged necessity for an equal value of the terms of exchange."[3] This is more than a change in point of view. It is a change in how we even think of a point of view and, to say the least, this has to change the way we talk about reality and write history. For it all looks different now and feels different too.

It is in this spirit that I wish to present a history of beauty in a small Colombian town, bearing in mind that Baudelaire claimed one could discern in clothing fashions "the moral and aesthetic feeling of their time."[4] Sure, it may seem a big jump from the splendor of mid-nineteenth-century Paris to a broken-down agribusiness town in the interior of Colombia in the second half of the twentieth century, but the aspiration and ambition to understand fashion in terms of the "feeling of the time" is the same and can be extended along with "drift" and Walter Benjamin's suggestion that "the collective dream energy of a society" takes refuge "in the mute impenetrable nebula of fashion, where the understanding cannot follow."[5]

Benjamin does hold out some hope for our understanding, however, when he further suggests that fashion is the "eternal deputy" of surrealism, which pitches fashion into art as well as into the uplift of "the marvellous"; something we can all do, if we so desire, pretty much every time we dress up to go out on the street. And like art, or at least one version of art, fashion is ahead of the curve of history. Although its prophetic signals are secret, Benjamin goes on to say,

Wendy Sulay Zuñiga Amu, 2009. Born and raised at the headwaters of the Timbiquí River on the Pacific coast of Colombia, she now resides in the city of Cali in the interior.

"whoever understands how to read these semaphores would know in advance not only about new currents in the arts but about new legal codes, wars, and revolutions."[6]

Maybe so, but in this maelstrom of secrecy and prophecy I feel the need to clutch at history—the history of beauty—in a small Colombian town. Yet no sooner do I write this than it sounds strange

Marina Grueso, life-long resident of Santa Barbara at the mouth of the
Timbiquí River, 2009.

to me. A history of beauty? What would that be? Is it restricted to
the human being or should it—must it—include the world around—
the streets, the buildings, the cultivated land, and the rivers? And if
it—this idea of a history of beauty—spreads like this, from the body
to the body of the world, if it is capacious, with these elements and
still others feeding into one another, then what of ugliness and what
of the moral quality of ugliness? When I look at the fetid rivers and
the crippled land, for instance, how can I split the moral from the
aesthetic?

A history of beauty? What would that be?

In 1972 I took photographs of women weeding the sugarcane
fields of the rich white guys who now own the valley. In those days,
before toxic herbicides were applied using tractors and small planes,
women were hired by labor contractors to do the weeding by hand.
You can see in the pictures that they are barefoot and extensively
covered despite the heat. They strike me as beautiful and outlandish, and, being outlandish, they haunt the scene, itself a cross sec-
tion through history with the peasant farms receding into the background of history as in the image itself. Wraiths in white, clutching

thick-handled shovels, they strike ungainly postures out of joint with history and with the land that was once theirs. Bodies askew, shovels at angles, old dresses tied to tasks for which dresses were never meant, they wear those tiny gold earrings from the old, old days that you rarely see anymore, visible here as tears of time.

A history of beauty? What would that be?

Weeding in the plantations was certainly harder than work on the traditional peasant farm, where even the tiny kids would accompany their mothers and you could sit and talk under the many species of trees that constitute these ecological miracles that are the traditional farm, replicas of the tropical rain forest at three thousand feet altitude, rooted in volcanic soil meters deep.

I wonder about my unthinking use of the phrase *work clothes*. For if I am not mistaken, work clothes are a luxury of the "advanced" societies such as North America, where stout men work with thick gloves and Timberland boots and cowboys are loaded down with leather chaps, metal-studded belts, and expensive hats. As I recall, the peasants I knew in 1970 did not have "work clothes." They worked wearing the same type of clothes they wore to town on Sundays, except the clothes were older.

Work seems the antithesis of beauty—a reflex opposition in a world that splits labor from leisure. But forty years down the track

we look back, and alongside drudgery we see a curious and powerful beauty in these photographs, inseparable from beauty and the
beast. Let me invoke that different world D. H. Lawrence describes,
the world of the miners and their families in the Derbyshire hills
around Nottingham, England, in the early twentieth century. As the
mines got deeper and the mining towns grew, an unspeakable ugliness spread across the land. "It was ugliness," he writes, "which be-

trayed the spirit of man, in the nineteenth century. The great crime which the moneyed classes and promoters of industry committed in the palmy Victorian days was the condemning of the workers to ugliness, ugliness, ugliness: meanness and ugly hope, ugly love, ugly clothes. . . . The human soul needs actual beauty even more than bread."

That was Lawrence. The miner's son.

The picture he paints is strange. It stays in my head. The miners' life is largely underground, like moles, scratching around in the semidarkness, seminude, bonding with each other, heaving and digging. They live by instinct and intuition and, unlike their womenfolk, love beauty for beauty's sake alone and not for love of possession. They cultivate flowers and are enchanted by the trembling notes they bring out of a piano with their rough hands, while for their nagging wives a piano in the house is merely a sign of status. Meanwhile, their houses and their towns are becoming increasingly horrible. Lawrence describes the architecture and town planning, but from the start he makes sure clothing and the making of clothing—work clothing—catches our eye, meaning our breath.

The memoir begins with a lyric description of the Derbyshire landscape as it was in the early days when Lawrence's grandather came to the town in the nineteenth century to make clothes for the miners of the B. W. & Co. mining company: "thick flannel vests, or singlets, and the moleskin trousers lined at the top with flannel, in which the colliers worked. I remember," he continues, "the great rolls of coarse flannel and pit cloth which stood in the corner of my grandfather's shop when I was a small boy, and the big, strange, old sewing machine, like nothing else on earth, which sewed the massive pit-trousers."[7]

This is Lawrence, the miner's son, and the overall sense you get

from him is that of the early twentieth-century world of production mercilessly closing down on the working class—so like and yet so unlike my town at the end of that century, where machines and chemicals have taken over the task of production and production has given way to consumption, where beauty in clothes and beauty in style, including music and dance, have become more and more pronounced while everything else becomes uglier and uglier. As with the morbid stories I hear about cosmic surgery, here beauty

lives side by side with murder and mutilation and is exacerbated by this ugliness. Similarly Lawrence's miners seem driven underground like moles, animals without light, ever more instinctual, ever more intuitive, ever more angry with their angry wives.

So the next "dialectical" or "dream image" in my history of beauty is quite surreal: these "moles" and that "big, strange, old sewing machine, like nothing else on earth, which sewed the massive pit-trousers." Perforce I am thinking of machines such as the windlass

Drawing by Olivia Taussig-Moore.

Lawrence describes, winding men down into the earth as well as the sewing machine that made their "prehistoric" work clothes. Perforce I am thinking of how all the women in the sugar plantation towns in Colombia until recently had sewing machines, so as to make beautiful clothes and furnishings for their familes and neighbors, and how the ever increasing pace of consumption has rendered such machines obsolete because people now buy their clothes off the rack. Made in China.

My friend Olivia Mostacilla, shown overleaf at her sewing machine, gave up making clothes at least ten years ago for this reason. For several years thereafter she walked the streets knocking on doors or badgering friends in this all-black town to buy clothes out of a smart catalog from a fashion house in Medellin displaying big-breasted white girls with blonde hair.

In upmarket areas of Berlin and London, in 2011, I saw branches of a fashionable clothing store chain whose expansive windows were stuffed, row upon row, with old sewing machines. Images of wildlife come to mind: herds of cattle on the run, a stampede of horses, geese flying south for the winter—this packed density of all-alike things, like the images of fire and cornfields and sand that Elias Canetti uses in *Crowds and Power* to get across the hushed sense of

the crowdness of crowds. At first I thought this might be some sort of antique store and ventured inside to ask if the machines were for sale, to be met with haughty indifference. No, they were not for sale. It was left for me to categorize them as objects of display, a historical joke, we might say, while inside the store the hipsters, none of whom could even thread a needle, were frenetically rifling through the expensive gray and black clothing.

Not for sale.

How curious. The machine that worked so well for so long, over a century, a commodity in itself, bought and sold across the world, itself producing other commodities, is not for sale. Not any more. It has become "art," in that zone where art copulates with commerce to provide the decor not for making clothes but for selling them. That which reproduced fashion has momentarily become fashion as fashion kills it off. These idle machines on the verge of extinction have been resuscitated as organic force, akin to a pack of wild animals, displayed not in a zoo but in a shop window.

I am rerouted to the outlandish again, to the *dialectical image* invoking prehistory—in this case the "prehistory" of those miners Lawrence evokes going down in a bucket into the bowels of the earth to work seminaked in the gloom, men of instinct and intuition as he ceaselesly reiterates, men dedicated, he says, to beauty.

It was Benjamin's intuition that by way of strange channels of emotion and remembrance of things lost, a danger in the present could usher in an image of something from the past, even the remote past, that would resonate with the present danger so as to create a montage of past and present. Crucial here is the interaction of history with nature, like the windlass winding down into and up from the earth. Such are these old photos of barefoot women weeding the cane fields, still-lifes outside of history that make history possible. There is a praxis here, the praxis of labor, meaning the interaction of body and mind and the material worked on. Body and earth fuse, as with Lawrence's almost naked miners, like moles, tunneling through the earth as natural habitat, only to emerge blinking in the light, and there to tickle the keys of the piano and cultivate pretty flowers. But there is fear and hatred too, if we turn to Lawrence's last published work, *Apocalypse,* in which he recalls from his childhood the ranting preachers in the Primitive Methodist chapels invoking the end of the world and the hoped-for destruction of the rich. "Strange marvellous black nights of the north Midlands, with the gas-light hissing in the chapel, and roaring of the strong-voiced colliers."[8] This is another form of praxis, political and cosmological. The more the worker goes underground working for the Man, the more certain the wrath of heaven. That is the praxis of heaven and hell, a cosmic battleground where I would also situate these women in the cane fields, the air thick with the shimmering heat. They are not naked underground like moles but animated streamers of time, decked out in layered and tattered clothes long since worn to shreds.

Which is why I want to push the idea of the dialectical image further, to read backward in order to read forward (in accord with the "secret" of fashion), as, for example, in the following photograph I took in my town in Colombia in 2009. Why this dreamy image in particular? Because it has the enigmatic quality of Benjamin's "semaphores" of fashion and because for me it exemplfies Lyotard's "drift" with its emphais on "affective intensity."

"Where have I come from?" this girl is asking. "Where am I going?" Her face is riveting as she pulls gently at her hair, which is not her hair at at all but an *extension*—false hair knitted into her real

hair—as if she is showing it off and thus confirming its existence. It is as if there is little existence anymore outside of display, she seems to be saying, or outside of the image displaying display. The hair is long, almost half as long as her body, and has a weblike lattice structure of knotted filaments that stand out against her thin white dress, the right side of which is flecked with gold.

"Where have I come from? Where am I going?"

Fashion is that which exists between past and future, a constantly shifting force field of collective dream energy, and that is why it has no history but continual erasure, which Benjamin marked as the death ritual of the commodity. But as we have already seen with the women in the cane fields and the sewing machines in the display windows, such a death is but prelude to another form of life transposed.

It is all very well to claim that fashion—those obscure "semaphores"—will alert you in advance about new legal codes, war, and revolution, but what if—what if ?—the wars and revolutions are forever, such that you are living your life in a permanent state of siege, a permanent state of "drift"? What then? What about fashion not *before* but *during* war and revolution? (Are not war and revolution subject to fashion too?) It is one thing to try to relate fashion to the prevailing state of society, culture, and morality. But it is quite another thing to contemplate the fashion for fashion when the aesthetics of everyday life swamp everyday life.

In such a situation of "drift," with its passion for *destape* and male prowess, as with a gun on a fast motorbike, what kind of surrealism are we to think of when Benjamin states that "fashion is the predecessor—no, the eternal deputy—of Surrealism"?[9] Are we talking Breton—or the scatologist Breton expelled, the Bataille of excess, that life in the fast lane we call *depense,* a behavior as much as a mode of thought, "whose *end* jumps the rails on which it is travelling"?[10]

For such a wide-ranging thinker, it is strange that Benjamin, with his idea of fashion as prophecy, never predicted the Nietzschean element in fashion—in youth fashion and in youth as fashion, the ultimate jumping off the rails. "Where are the young people, where are the elements of surprise?" asks an editor at the fashion magazine *Elle,* while watching the uptight Givenchy show of the 2010 spring collections in Paris.[11] Well, the young people may not have been at that particular fashion show, but they have certainly stepped into the fashion show of world history, and with untold elements of surprise. Hegel and Marx would be dumbfounded at this explosion of Eros and Dionysus and its impact on the World Spirit previously directed toward the gods of Reason and Revolution.

history of
the shoe

NO SHIRT, NO SHOES, NO SERVICE! What is is about bare feet that
drives man crazy and makes shoes the granddaddy of all fetishes? Ex-
planations abound but fall short of the emotional tumult, although
Bataille got close with a remarkable essay on the adventures of the
big toe. For according to him, all of Hegel, Marx, and Nietzsche are
there in that appendage slugging it out. The way it works is this: The
human body lends itself to allegories (and hence cosmic surgery),
especially those allegories that deem the head superior, the emperor
of our being, while the foot is that far-flung colonial outpost, that
imbecilic base on which—it has to be admitted—the rest of the body,
including the emperor, depends. It is this "has to be admitted" that
is the problem, which for Bataille is the irreconcilability of these
interdependent entities—the mighty head, the humble foot—an irreconcilability that fatefully removes us from the safe and elegant
certainties of dialectical spinning wheels and instead plunges us into
a maelstrom in which laughter no less than tears runs amuck.

What a shock (therefore) it was for me in 1970 to step into the
barefoot peasant world of Puerto Tejada direct from London and
Bogotá, and at the same time to come to grips with the fact that
it was profoundly important to be dressed right (and then, twenty
years later, to see the rules for what was right turned inside out). I
recall how María Cruz Zappe, leaning barefoot on her crutch poking wood into the cooking fire in her bamboo and mud hut, would

not allow her five-year-old grandson to go to the hospital because
he had no shoes.

The mysterious German-Mexican writer B. Traven has a story, *The
Bridge in the Jungle*, in which a bracero working in Texas in the 1920s
returns to his village in Chiapas, southern Mexico, with a present

for his kid brother—"a pair of genuine American shoes. The soles of these shoes were polished and they were smooth as glass. Carlosito, of course, had to put on his new shoes to show the giver how much he liked them. Never before in his life had he worn shoes on his feet."[1] That night, playing on the oil company's bridge in the dark during a *fiesta*, Carlos falls to his death in the river. He falls because he normally goes barefoot and is not used to shoes. The *fiesta* stops and people drag the river but can't find the body until they resort to magic, using a floating candle that bobs up and down over the body. They find the body, the *fiesta* resumes, and later the boy is buried. On the way to the graveyard the brass band plays "Yes! We Have No Bananas."

Which is more magical, the use (and success) of the candle, or the gift of the shoes to the previously barefoot boy?

Traven's story anticipates the role of the shoe in shaping modern culture. So why does the boy have to die?

Women working for the wealthy landowners in the 1970s around my town in western Colombia would work barefoot, placing fearsome chemicals by hand onto each fledgling corn plant, one plant at a time, an unbelievable sight. Bare feet. Bare hands. And try to imagine the burning heat. In the background wherever there are trees, you can see the remaining peasant farms, archaeological traces

of the time before time. Two men are driving the barefoot women from behind. One woman stands erect, perhaps to ease her back. Her stance is resolute, yet she seems lost for the moment, a figure out of time grasping at a vision, her right hand gripping a bottle of chemicals, her feet gripping the soil.

Women weeding sugarcane on the plantations at that time were likewise barefoot, as were women in the peasant plots shelling cacao grown on their own land.

But not the young men of today. No way. Goodbye bare foot. Hello Nike, hello Reebok ...

It was little short of a revolution when rubber boots came in the 1970s. *Croydon*, they were called. The Colombia guerrilla, the FARC, drawn overwhelmingly from the peasantry of central Colombia, from regions such as Huila, Cauca, and Tolima, were quick to get themselves rubber boots—sign of a peasant army—while the US-

funded army of the state boasts shiny black leather boots. Thus did the shoe enter the technology of war.

Then came the other side of work and war, not the sweaty rubber boot but the sneaker, the God-given sneaker put on this earth for luxury and *depense*—and how much *depense!* The floodgates of desire opened. Motorbikes, fragmentation grenades, and sexual display notwithstanding, it is doubtful that the world has known a device as desired as the sneaker, real or faux, bought in a store for outrageous sums of money or stolen or stripped off a still-bleeding corpse. Let us recall that rare and delightful bird in flight we spied earlier. Not the Rolls Royce rolling down the avenues of Manhattan but its everyman's equivalent, the men's shoe winking at me from behind glass in the airport at Bogotá, with a price tag of 290 US dollars.

Who could explain such unquenchable desire for a shoe—a mere shoe, as if it is precisely here that beauty and utility achieve the perfect union.

In this vein, does not the opposition of boot to sneaker reflect the pairing, if not the conflict, between hard labor and the awesome glow of the fetish? You see the women in the 1970s photographs working barefoot in the corn fields of the rich. You seem them barefoot in the cane fields of the rich. You see them barefoot shelling cacao. They are so formidable, these women, especially when working with their extended families shelling cacao grown on their own land, which might better be called their garden. Labor is what these images evince, while the image of the young dudes speaks another language altogether, the language of exhibition. The young men in this photograph are so damn cool. Another beauty is born.

Put aside the invention of the steam engine and the spinning jenny. The history I have in mind is somewhat older, concerning the invention of bipedal locomotion and with that a slew of meanings concerning the relation of foot to face and the evolution of beauty.

This is the history of the ascent of man, that noble animal, teetering forth like a newborn on two and not four legs. Nietzsche gives us the big picture, and Freud focuses it. Nietzsche evokes "the sea animals when they were forced to become either land animals or perish—at one go, all instncts were devalued and 'suspended.' Now they had to walk on their paws and 'carry themselves' whereas before they had been carried by the water. "A terrible heaviness bore down on them."[2] To Nietzsche this is the heaviness of repression that, thwarting the instincts, turns them inward to form the soul. Quite an achievement. But it is the foot that will bear the weight.

Like Nietzsche, Freud tied this evolutionary moment, when man stood erect, to the birth of civilization and its discontents. The vertical axis of foot and head became not only the template of thought and reality but the allegory of the cosmos itself. Now vision replaced smell and touch (as Nietzshe's Apollo displaces Dionysus) and, above all, shame at the now-exposed genitalia entered the world. Clothing was created to cover the offending organs, and smell—the demoted sense—became the sign of repression, no less, it appears, than the foot itself.[3]

But now *Civilization and Its Discontents* has to be rewritten. The girls have taken off their clothes, their mothers wail *destape!*, and the boys no longer follow the dictates of the fathers, who seem old beyond years, even quaint. Dionysus has returned, resplendent in Nike shoes like winged sandals of yore, recalling Nietzsche's question as to whether a "reverse experiment" is in principle possible? But, he adds, "who has sufficient strength?" Well, we know the answer, meaning the young people of the agribusiness slum towns and hamlets—especially given that Nietzsche heatedly asks this question because a simple reversal, a simple denial of denial, is neither simple nor easy, because reversal is too bound up with the perverse features of the bad conscience of "civilization" that perforce enters into the reversal itself. "We would need another sort of spirit," he says, "spirits which are strengthened by wars and victories, for which conquest, adventure, danger and even pain have actually become a necessity." They would need, he concludes, "a sort of sublime nastiness."[4]

Bare feet become shod is one history, an undeniably practical, down-to-earth, basely material story with some nice evolutionary uplift: from the heavy mud of rain-sodden fields clinging to your ankles, or the dust of summer between your toes, to the smelly comfort of those sweaty rubber boots. The splayed bare feet with the big toe curling outward like a claw as you get older became a relic, something you might find in a natural history museum of bygone freaks, far from the coolness of the dudes in their sneakers.

But what of the head? Has it not also experienced momentous changes? Take the surreal playground of hair in recent years, that epitome of the nonpractical, of excess heaped on excess—the overflowing abundance of flow, expensive and wondrous, accompanying the revelation of more and more of the body. I refer to women, with their fantastic hair extensions, like the snakes entwined in the hair of Dionysus's Maenads. But I could with a snap of the finger be referring to the men, who now have it all off, leaving a burnished bald skull glowing in the surreal game as well. It seems like overnight the human species has gone and altered itself in some fantastic mutation. For it all looks different now, and it all feels different now.

As men's hair got shorter and then disappeared, women—including girls as young as four or five—started to have extensions stitched into theirs, descending in great waves to the midback. Inserting these extensions takes at least an hour and is not cheap, and the hair lasts at most two months before it gets lank and greasy. But is that not the point—to expend, to practice some *depense*, to set it flowing?

This play with hair lends itself to all sorts of games with history and with the meaning of signs, but I want to mention first the intimacy— the intimacy of having other women graft extensions into your real hair or straighten it, with yet other women close by, watching, touching, talking, while those deft fingers splice their knots and webs.

As for history and the dialectical image, how could one ignore the fantastic hair sculpture in Africa, for men as well as for women.

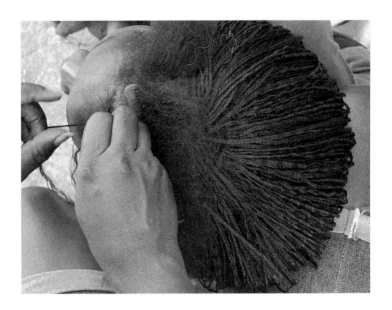

The practice seems very old, certainly as old as the colonial record, and includes extensions that reach the ground, as shown in a 1940s photograph taken in Namibia[5].

When I first came to my town in Colombia in late 1969, black women's hair was short, worn in tiny cornrows, braided, or straightened using herbal mixtures sold in tubes of bamboo and made, so it was said, by Indians from plants. Or else a broken machete, hot and greased with fat from the hoof of a cow, might be applied to the hair. Back then the town had some twelve thousand inhabitants and but one *sala de belleza*, and that was the proprietor's living room. Around that time expensive hair-straightening ointments from the United States started to be used, and most of the younger women used curlers—actually the cardboard cylinders from rolls of toilet paper—to create waves in their straigthened hair. These were worn for days, it seemed, inside the house and out in the street, such that it seemed natural, like hair itself. Can you imagine, the street bobbing with toilet paper rolls! Later, brightly colored plastic rollers were used, bright blues and yellows, for instance, which like the cardboard rollers, became, to my eyes at least, beautifying adornments in themselves and not merely means to having straightened hair. Today, all that has disappeared, with hair-straightening lotions and the gentle

Photo by K. Shettler. From *Hair-styles, Head-dresses, and Ornaments in Southwest Africa, Namibia and Southern Angola*, ed. A. Scherz et al. (Windhoek: Gamsberg Macmillan, 1981).

ministrations of goddesses such as Nima who pamper the ladies in their salons, this same lovely Nima who cuts my hair with her hair down to her waist, lustrous, brown, and mainly false.

Along with *destape* and the radical change in hair, there is this other landscape of change, the nonhuman landscape of trauma and burnished skull, violence and the unremitting ugliness of slum dwellings and agribusiness plantations stretching to what used to be the horizon but now extends far beyond the limits of the known

world. Guarding these limits that are not limits at all you find the fantastic new machinery imported to harvest sugarcane, a salute to the tens of thousands of cane-cutters being laid off, a sign that the rationalization of the land by the machine is now complete. With this triumph, the machines do nothing if not evoke prehistory.

And the kids? As the ugliness spreads and the streets go crazy with violence and wild stories thereof, so the kids become daring and skillfull at being beautiful, turning themselves into works of art in a world aimed at eliminating them as they eliminate each other.

surgeons of the underworld

COSMIC SURGERY EXISTS IN A BREACH OF REALITY into which floods the incandescence of the fairy tale. How incredible it all is. To be remade like that. To make the world more 90-60-90. Agribusiness has transformed the landscape of the earth and rivers, and now cosmic surgery transforms the body of woman. Yet how dangerous too! For have not women's bodies become a type of agribusiness, along with monocropping, artificial fertilizers, dangerous pesticides, and irrigation? And has not nature struck back, as my stories instruct? That woman in the dark, hot room, in a coma after *la lipo*, the woman who can't close her eyes, the woman breathing like a cat, those double mastectomies and liters of pus drained from each buttock.

How dangerous it has all become. Not just dangerous but unreal, inflamed by the supernatural force that runs through tales of transformation, of treasure sought, of kingdoms lost and giants slain. Not just dangerous but unreal, as in theater and masquerade, where police connive with gangsters, presidents with paramilitaries, and corruption fertilizes the killing fields to such an extent and with such diabolical insinuations that you never know who or what to believe. It is indeed the baroque, wherein an aesthetic of artificiality and the inordinate complexity of statecraft theatricalizes the world—nowhere more so than in the tales of larger-than-life criminals subject to cosmic surgery.

That the fairy tale enjoys an exuberant life in the daily news was brought out many years ago in the back room of a bookstore in Paris on rue Gay-Lussac where, under the clouds of imminent war, a small group of writers and anthropologists met to discuss what they called "sacred sociology." Acrimoniously ejected from Andre Breton's surrealists, they formed their own magazines and venues, such as the one Roger Caillois addressed in 1939 with a dazzling talk entitled "The Sociology of the Executioner."[1]

Like James Joyce describing one day in the mind of a hapless Jew in Dublin, Caillois takes one day in the mind of the daily press, February 2, 1939, as it reports on the death of the French Republic's executioner, seventy-six-year-old Anatole Deibler.

Callois delivered this talk but three years after the publication of Walter Benjamin's "The Storyteller," an essay in which newspapers are held to cause a decline in storytelling, trafficking as they do in information rather than stories. While Benjamin laments what he sees as the demise of storytelling, "sacred sociologists" like Caillois had a more nuanced view, in which even the news article could be colored by the fairy tale or serve as a storehouse of facts for storytellers' use, something for Benjamin to ruminate upon as he sat shaking his head in perplexity in the back rows of the their discussions in a Paris bookstore. At least that's the story.

What Caillois perceived in the cascade of news articles concerning the death of the executioner was a world of myth and legend binding the executioner to the king, "one in brilliance and splendor and the other in darkness and shame." Both king and executioner are exceptional beings who seem close together yet also far apart, such that we tend to "identify with them and to draw back from them at the same time, in one movement of avidity and repulsion":

We have already acknowledged the psychological constellation defining man's attitude when confronted with the sacred. It is described by Saint Augustine who confesses how he burns with ardor when he thinks of his resemblance to the divine, and shudders with horror when he recalls how different he remains from it.[2]

According to the newspapers, the executioner Deibler was a shy, tranquil man, in love with his little dog and card games. Like the king, he is a supernatural being, full of contradiction. The man who instills fear is himself afraid. Since childhood he has lived apart from people. Brutal as is his profession, his face is said to be that of a sweet, melancholic man. His villa is said to resemble a blockhouse on the Maginot line, yet he cultivates roses. Said to live in areas of the city frequented by criminals and prostitutes, he is credited with the powers of sorcery and healing.

"The executioner touches both worlds," notes Cailllois, with a wealth of alusion and felicity of phrase. "His mandate is from the law, but he is the last of its servants, the one nearest the dark, peripheral regions where the very ones he is fighting stir and hide. He seems to emerge from a terrible, disordered zone into the light of order and legality."[3]

In this manner the executioner fulsomely illustrates not only his magical connections with the criminal, but also the dependence of the sovereign on the criminal. This sublime connection means that at times the criminal manifests the attributes of royalty, a point made much of by Jean Genet in his *Thief's Journal*, as when he tells us of the criminal with the amputated hand with whom he wants to make love. This is handsome, aloof, and avowedly straight Stilitano, who abases himself in a Barcelona street one night. Having insulted three guys, he backs down from a fight when they turn on him. He pathetically holds out his stump toward them. "The absence of the hand," writes Genet, "was as real and effective as a royal attribute, as the hand of justice."[4]

Great criminals assume mythic powers equal to those of the sovereign and his police. Take the magical metamorphoses in the underworld, as illustrated in the picture of a notorious criminal published in 2007 in Colombia's main newspaper, *El Tiempo,* when it announced unexpected news in a strangely paster-than-past tense, so past it sounded like *Once upon a time. . .*

THUS FELL "CHUPETA," THE CAPO OF SIX SURGERIES[5]

Immediately below the headline and stretching the entire width of the page was a horizontal strip of black and white photographs of six distinct faces not much bigger than a postage stamp, one next to the other forming a chronological series entitled "The Metamorphosis."

The first photo showed Chupeta as a handsome young man with

El Tiempo, August 8, 2007.

an intense, narrow face, pursed lips, black shiny hair brushed straight back, and unblemished skin. He could be a model for hair oil. This is how he looked in 1996 when he did a deal with the law confessing to trafficking thirty tons of cocaine in exchange for just four years in prison. Later the newspaper reported that the ever-reliable US Department of Drug Enforcement claimed Chupeta shipped out seven hundred tons.

Around this time his partner, "The Razor," was assassinated, and six months after his release from jail, Chupeta went into hiding because a court in Washington had issued an order for his capture to stand trial in the United States. Soon thereafter his right-hand man, Laureano Rentería, was poisoned with cyanide and died in his prison cell a few days before he was to meet with US authorities armed with the power of extradition.

When he was caught by the police a second time, in 2008, Chupeta was reported to have a fortune stashed away, as well as having had himself "stashed away," so to speak, thanks to a new face and a number of other transformations—including his alleged death and, in preparation for his resurrection, new names and passports, and still more cosmic surgery.

Through a plant in the Colombian army he had spread the rumor that he was dead. Meanwhile, surgeons got busy on his face, and perhaps also his fingerprints, as he traveled to Mexico, Paraguay, Uruguay, Argentina, and Brazil, where, some time between 2005 and 2007, he settled down as an Italian by name of Marcelo Javier Unzue.

No less dramatic than death, real or phony, are the sequential instantiations of this man, or should I say, this face, on the run. Indeed, the sequence of images, read left to right, suggests a cycle of death and resurrection, each rebirth more sinister. What is it that makes us cringe? Is it that the face gets more and more screwed up—uglier, nastier, scarier? Is it the painful recognition that someone allowed this to happen to his face and hence, so we might suppose, to his very being? Is that what fascinates—the mere fact of change in what we once thought unchangeable, namely the human face, mooring of identity?

"I feel betrayed," moaned the eminent São Paulo plastic surgeon Lorití Breuel, who had in all innocence performed the three most recent operations. She had only just learned, she said, the true identity of her patient, who had, she was told, ordered more than three hundred assassinations. "But he was so *simpático*," she wailed. Her staff is swallowing tranquilizers to deal with the shock.

Well, who wouldn't feel betrayed? Look at that final work of art, a no-face, a grotesque excuse for a face, a carnival mask of broad flat planes, eyes bulging scary white like golf balls, and a taut smile, more like a grimace of constant pain.

What gave him away, finally, was his voice, samples of which were fed into what *El Tiempo* calls the "voice bank" maintained by the US Drug Enforcement Agency. Thus was his identity confirmed. The face is spectacularly the guarantor of identity and much else besides. But that invisible entity, one's voice, is no less so. How strange that we rarely recognize or approve of our own voice, remaining strangers to our vocal selves, but not to an old friend, to the DEA. When will cosmic surgeons attend to the voice? Or rather, when will our awareness of personal beauty and its possibilities for change extend to the possibilities of voice?

Stimulated by the capture of Chupeta, *El Tiempo* provided a few days later the headline introducing a page of stories about a shadowy world of "surgeons" who are busy— the world over, so it seems—changing the identities of people sought by the police. They "operate" not only in clinics but in the filing systems of state intelligence services such as the DAS and DJIN, erasing and replacing records. As for what DAS and DJIN are, best you not ask.

According to this article, microsurgery on one's fingerprints is an obsession among bad guys, and consequently among the police. Some surgeons delicately "rewrite" the whorls of the fingers, others mutilate them to leave no usable print, while still others are said to exchange a person's toe prints with their fingerprints. Less technical methods exist as well. The case is cited of a desperate man in Bogotá who chewed off his fingertips so as to evade detection. But that is nothing compared with the woman who cut off the forefinger of her dead husband, storing it in the freezer so she could use it to withdraw his monthly pension.

Two years later a paramilitary killer by the name of Pedro Julio Rueda came forth with a rather surprising account of fingerprint surgery.[6] Together with an unnamed number of others active in the Bloque Centauros on the great plains of Colombia spreading east toward Venezuela, he claimed to have had the fingerprints of a peasant captured by the paramilitaries grafted onto his fingers. The grafts were performed in primitive conditions, he explained: a deep cut was made into each of his fingers ("as deep as the tendons"), then sections of the fingertips of the peasant were laid into the hollows. It was necessary to kill three or four captives to get this right, but they would have killed more had it been necessary.

The experiment, however, proved a failure, leaving Rueda with no fingerprints at all and deep scars that caused much pain when he attended to what are delicately described as his basic needs. It was five or six months before he could again hold a gun.

And what about Amado Carrillo, the Mexican drug king known as *el señor de los cielos*—"master of the heavens," a reference, no doubt, to his fleet of jet planes flying drugs into the USA as much as to his godlike wealth and power. In July 1997 Carrillo died under the knife of not one but three plastic surgeons, including the Colombian Ricardo Reyes Rincón. The operation to change *el señor de los cielos* is said to have lasted eight hours, with one surgeon working on the nose while the other got into some radical liposuction to reduce his abdominal fat. A few days later, the three surgeons were found dead, according to *El Tiempo,* but closer study suggests that only two of them were found, dead, very dead, encased in cement, blindfolded and handcuffed, showing signs of having been burned, battered, and strangled.

There are two images of the face of this *el señor de los cielos* in the Wikipedia article I consulted. The first is a portrait reminscent of a young Jesus, with falling locks and beard, sweet and noble, soberly colored in brown shaded black and white. The second, in unsettling, repellent colors, is a side view of the head, post–plastic surgery, in a coffin, bolstered by capacious white pillowy stuff. The skin is a mottled pink with purple spots. The gums are bared, showing prominent teeth. Divinity has taken a dive. Beauty knows no sadder fate than this fall to bestiality, from which no redemption seems possible other than the shudder of a good story.

the designer name

"ALL THAT IS LEFT IS YOUR NAME."

Is there not a parallel between cosmic surgery and naming, or rather renaming? Just as your face and body root your identity, so of course does your name. Hence, to take another name or to be renamed—as by a nickname or alias—would seem no less a metaphysical shift in one's being than that performed by cosmic surgery. How naming and cosmic surgery converge is nowhere more apparent, and indeed frightening, than in the case of the killers and swindlers swelling the leadership of the Colombian paramilitaries, mere stooges, of course, for the invisible persons behind them, unnamed and with neither face nor body. Nor should the humor be lost on us, the humor that makes the terror all the more terrifying.

Mafia Naming

Take the name Chupeta, the name of "the capo of six surgeries" and of a candy sold in Colombia, *chupar* being a word meaning "to suck." Straightforward as this connection might appear, it took me some time to hear it spelled out. People I asked assumed the nickname must have deeper significance, something secret, something strange, belonging to the misty recesses of the criminal underworld and therefore indecipherable, as if such names must always mean more.

In other words, the meaning of such names refers us to the meaning of naming, indicating a surplus, a penumbra of inaccessibility that Bataille would surely deem *depense,* meaning unprofitable expenditure, along with poetry and play. For nicknames are a slippery lot, nowhere more so than with regards to the naming of gangsters. Freud's analysis of jokes and their relation to the unconscious comes to mind because such names, it seems to me, are meant to play with meanings and double meanings, as well as with the notion of concealment. It is as if the slipperiness of those sliding, double meanings reflects the cloak-and-dagger lives the criminal is thought to lead.

There is a lot of confusion about what to call such names. Are they *nicknames* or are they *aliases?* For while the former, like the term *sobriquet,* suggests a degree of conviviality, camaraderie, and humor; the latter belongs more to the lexicon of the police, ever ready to tear away at the patina of innocence with which a name enshrouds our being. An alias tends to act as camouflage, to be as undistinguished as possible (e.g., Jack Smith), while a nickname is theatrical, a flashing light intended, for one reason or another, to stand out. An alias is a "real" name, like Jack Smith or Jane Brown, while a nickname stands askew from such names, as if to mock them and make you think twice about naming itself. My favorite appellation, however, is the *nom de guerre,* a supercharged hybrid of alias and nickname wrapped in a generous swath of cloak-and-dagger, while pseudonyms, such as mine, Mateo Mina, raise another form of reference altogether. All these forms of naming naming suggest a wondrously complex world of doubling identities and masking. And while the parallel with cosmic surgery should not be lost on us, nor should this complexity.

Nicknames power up the ordinary world by adding a rough-edged humor, mystery, and theater. They combine the familiar with the remote, as with that fool, El Loco Barrera, "the man most wanted in the nation." How cartoonlike and melodramatic, yet frighteningly real, this can be is brought out when we read of El Loco's one thousand bodyguards, under the command of Pedro Oliverio Guerrero, alias Cuchillo, The Knife, a paramilitary chieftan who led "the Heroes of Vichada," another name to contend with.

The Heroes of Vichada. Tell me this is not as funny as it is terrifying. Eduardo Vanegas, who served time in the Colombian army before turning to the anthropological study of massacres in northern

Colombia, tells me they are actually the Heroes of Guviare, but at any rate they are heroes, even if their names swirl in a delirium of nomenclature. "Pity the country that needs heroes," Brecht famously wrote. In what name can we now believe, especially since they are now, these heroes, called ERPAC (pronunced *ur-pack*), which is even more cartoonish when you get the full blast: Ejercito Revolucionario Antisubversivo de Colombia (Popular Revolutionary Antisubversive Army of Colombia). ERPAC is allegedly allied with Los Aguilas Negras, "the Black Eagles." What fun it must be to coin these names, and how agonizing it must be to reach that fork in the road of creative naming where you have to choose between mind-numbing bureaucratese, as with ERPAC, and the gangsta, comic-book style of Black Eagles?

Then there is Cadena—meaning "chain," meaning gold chain, meaning gold necklaces and bracelets—which, as a nickname barely competes with its bearer's real name, Rodrigo Mercado Pelufo. He was one of the paramilitary leaders of the Heroes of Montes de María, referring to one the more spectacularly violent areas of Colombia, near the Caribbean coast, where in in just two years, 1999 and 2000, the Heroes massacred entire villages such as El Salado, Chengue, and Macayepo—seventy-five villages in all. Some three thousand people were killed or disappeared.

Cadena was involved in these massacres and was said to have been himself assasinated sometime in 2004 or 2005 because he was ready to reveal the names of the landlords and politicians who supported the aforesaid Heroes. Thus his alias, *chain*, acquired yet another allusion, that of the invisible chain of command leading up to who knows where, perhaps, so it is said, to the the office of the then-president. In this sense, the chains of gold that bestowed upon him a shining mantle of *depense* appear to have also killed him. Other stories in the region recount other excesses, such as the torture room in one of his haciendas called *el cuarto de las ultimas lagrimas*, "the room of one's last tears." Situated in the basement, this dungeon was said to have had a pool full of alligators. García Marquez and magical realism can scarcely compete.

As for El Loco, who could ever be sure of his "real" name; at last count he had three state-generated IDs, one of which bears the number 79.947.575. Newspapers are certainly generous with information. Said to be the "most-wanted man in the nation," he is described in the newspaper *El Espectador* as a drug kingpin who bought cocaine and cocaine paste from paramilitaries as well as from John 40, second in command of the forty-third front of the FARC guerrilla, deadly enemy of the paramilitaries, with whom, nevertheless, they do business.[1]

(Take note also of Jorge 40—not John 40—who was one of the best-known paramilitary leaders and whose real name (if there is such a thing anymore) is Rodrigo Tovar Pupo. So we have John 40, the guerrilla leader openly selling cocaine in huge amounts on behalf of the guerrilla to the paramilitary enemy, and we also have fat, bespectacled Jorge 40, a nice boy from one of the best families in Valledupar, now posing for photo-ops with his weapon and a sweaty band of camouflaged paramilitary desperadoes at war with the likes of John 40. It is so confusing. What if you mistook John 40 for Jorge 40?)

In the colored photographs supplied by the national police to the daily newspaper it seems that the cosmic surgeons did a nice job on Daniel Barrera. He was so ugly before, what with his arrogant mouth, bulbous eyes, and fleshy, overweight face—like a grouper cornered in a cave in an ocean reef. Over the course of eight months he was subject to so much cosmic surgery, including liposuction, that "according to some informants he has become practically unrecognizable."[2] He has lost more than sixty pounds. And that's not all he has lost. His fingerprints have mysteriously disappeared from the State Registry, as has the original of the photograph I show here. So much for El Loco, or what used to be El Loco, whom I will rename The Grouper.

Comparativo de Daniel 'El Loco' Barrera y Juan Barrera Fonseca. Cortesía Noticias Uno.

El Espectador, August 14, 2008.

Paramilitary Naming

Then there is that other Daniel, also a paramilitary, Daniel Rendón Herrera, known as Don Mario and also as El Paisano, originally the right-hand man of his paramilitary brother Fredy, known as El Alemán (the German) on account of the strict discipline he imposed on his unruly pack of torturers and killers. Captured by the Colombian army on April 16, 2009, don Mario was famous "for his passion for vintage brandy and designer suits. He was rumoured to use $100 bills to light cigars, and liked to wear a new Rolex every day."[3] What a character! Larger than life, stereotype of a sterotype, how could such a fellow be content with an ordinary name, a "real" name?

Alongside this plethora of nicknames we have the practice of *no-names*. In 2007 I received news that the eight paramilitary leaders considered most responsible for seizing the land of four million Colombians are frustrated at not being able to publicly name the people for whom they kill and torture and from whom they receive payment and protection. These eight did a deal with the president of the republic for a modified amnesty, provided they repent their sins in public and disclose the secrets of their organizations. But there are secrets and there are secrets. The president decided he didn't want them to say a word more, and now they have been muzzled or sent off to prison in the United States on drug charges, which is the same as being muzzled. They subsequently wrote a collective letter stating that they need to talk, that their demobilization and disarmament is worthless if those nice people at the top of society who call the shots remain invisible. Otherwise paramilitary organizations will simply reproduce.[4] They say that they themselves are merely "the tip of the iceberg," merely the "shock troops." That is their argument. But of course it is also a threat. Give us a better deal or we will talk!

Below their signatures they put their fingerprints.

Here is the list of names provided the reader: Fredy Rendón, a.k.a. El Alemán, Rodrigo Pérez (Julián Bolívar), Arnubio Triana (Botalón), Jorge Iván Laverde (El Iguano), Álvaro Sepúlveda (Don César), Edwar Cobos (Diego Vecino), Jesús Ignacio Roldán (Monoleche), and Raúl Emilio Hasbún (Pedro Bonito).

The journalist who provides this information fails to make clear whether it is she who has supplied each nom de guerre or whether this was done by the letter writers themselves. In either case, I assume these "names of war" are as well known as their "real names." Or better known. It's gotten to the stage where it would seem indecent not to present both names together, not "Fredy Rendón"—that would seem a little too familiar—but the full appellation, "Fredy Rendón (El Alemán)." These are hybrid figures, like centaurs or like a musical score in which each iteration of a given note is accompanied by another note, as in the calls of certain birds and cell phones.

There is a fascinating structure here: the hybrid names up front, and behind them, the no-names—a governor, a large landowner, a cabinet minister, a US embassy official, or even the president. The visible tip of the iceberg and the larger, submerged mass, hidden in the frigid depths. It is as if the man with his hybrid name is actually carrying a name for his nameless benefactor.

Guerrilla Naming

The enemies of the paramilitaries, the guerrilla leaders of the FARC, may change their names too, although in keeping with their sobriety, as well as the logic of an alias, they favor everyday names like Manuel Marulanda (from Pedro Antonio Marín), Jacobo Arenas (Luís Morantes), Raúl Reyes (Luis Edgar Devia Silva), Alfonso Cano (Guillermo Sáenz), and Simón Trinidad, a.k.a. Federico Bogotá, whose original, or should I say "real," name was ever so much more inventive: Juvenal Ovidio Ricardo Palmera Pineda. There he was, running a big bank in Valledupar in the north of Colombia, married to another big banker, lovely respectable people, when one day in 1987 he lit off to the hills of the Serranía de Perijá to form Frente 41 of the FARC, with thirty million pesos from the bank plus details of the bank accounts of the town's wealthiest burghers—useful information for later kidnappings.

This switch in names and vocation seems as sudden and dramatic a change of identity as one could wish. Lest we forget, just before Simón Trinidad took off with their millions, the burghers of Valledupar and like-minded landowners throughout the country were organizing the elimination of the newly created Unión Patriótica party, which they claimed was a legal front of the FARC. Ably assisted by their paramilitary units, the Colombian army, and drug lords like El Mexicano, José Gonzalo Rodriguez Gacha, they were pretty successful. Within a few years there were no UP members of importance left in Colombia. One by one they had been assassinated, several thousand of them.

Lower-echelon guerrilla fighters may get names according to a quite different system. One such fighter is identified only as Desconfianza (Suspicious, or the Skeptic) in the tape-recorded interviews he had with Alfredo Molano concerning the important role he played in the Colombian Communist Party and its guerrilla army, the FARC. He is otherwise unnamed by Molano to avoid making him easier to track down and kill. He was in the guerrilla from its earliest days in the 1960s, and before that he served as bodyguard of the now legendary Juan de la Cruz Varela—which is a real name, John of the Cross Varela—an astonishing man, a rarity without nickname or alias. But those were early days and it would take a lot of nerve to change such a beautiful name as Juan de la Cruz Varela.

A name like Desconfianza, by contrast, makes you wonder about names that are not just an alias, like Manuel Marulanda, but instead reflect character or point to a story. In his taciturn way, Desconfianza points out that sometimes you choose the name but other times it chooses you.[5]

The most endearing account I have come across of getting an alias or a nickname (or is it a nom de guerre?) was that of a FARC member who chose her own name, Melisa. Deep in the mountains of southern Colombia, having satisfied the guerrilla comandante that she was tough, smart, and trustworthy, she was given her equipment: a small cooking pot, a spoon, a "house," meaning a thick plastic sheet, and an "iron" (*fierro*), meaning a gun, which in her case was named—or nicknamed—El Pierna de Pisco on account of its long muzzle.

So not only people are named and renamed. Guns are too. That rather important piece of Melisa's equipment, her "piece," is not only euphemized as *un fierro*, but on top of that receives a second name, or metaname, and God knows how that stranger than strange name originated. The revolution may have failed so far, but the language shows promise.

As her gun was handed over she was at the same time asked what name she wanted for herself? Without thinking twice she said Melisa, "because I so admired Melissa Gilbert, who played the part of Laura in *La familia Ingalls*, a TV program I adored. I liked her because of her subtle smile that conveyed the sense of a dream. But afterward they gave me a nickname I hated, Cacharina."[6] This was the name of the corn mash she had to make for the guerrilla group each morning, after she was taken out of combat to serve as cook, which she loathed.

Guerrilla leaders may be blessed with more than one type of alternate name, for not only is there the change from one conventional name to another conventional name (from Pedro Antonio Marín to Manuel Marulanda), but some have in addition a nickname and a nom de guerre, and thus belong to the same poetic universe of naming we find among criminals and paramilitaries.

Melisa becomes Cacharina, just as Marulanda, for decades the leader of the FARC guerrilla army, carries the nickname of Tirofijo or "Sure Shot," but my sense is that this name was bestowed by his enemies, not by the guerrila itself, although it came to be used by them as well, I believe. It is a fun name with a measure of respect, testimony to the notion that we are enthralled by larger-than-life persons who become personages on account of their taking over from the state the function of making law.

Nicknames make you ask questions you wouldn't ask of an "ordinary" or real name. Nicknames open up names and the act of naming. They splay language open so as to provide alternate universes, stepping out of the rut of everyday life. Having a nickname or an alias is like having a mask, a cover over the real face, similar to what a facelift provides. We should note—surely it is of historic significance?—that only recently have masks come back in fashion, along with facelifts. There has to be a subterranean connection beween Botox and those Russian police in dark balaclavas manhandling some fearful Chechnyan or beating up demonstrators and journalists in Georgia, where Stalin was born. Now, he never wore a mask, although Stalin—meaning "steel man"—was his nickname, I mean nom de guerre, or was it an alias? And certainly such a name is as good as a mask. In the US for a while he was Uncle Joe.

To change one's identity via cosmic surgery or via a new name or a nickname is equivalent to dying and being reborn. This can occur without actually dying, as in the case of Chupeta, but it can also occur when a person has died and his followers attempt to mask the fact, if it is a fact. Sometimes you never know, and that is the beauty of this strategy, which was tried by the inner circle around the legendary Colombian guerrilla leader Manuel Marulanda.

For at least three or four years up to the time I write these lines, in 2007, it has been put about that Marulanda is dead or terminally ill. Given deliberate obfuscation by both the Colombian state and the guerrilla, given the secrecy, fear, ferocious armed struggle, lies, and multiple levels of deceit and theatricality on both sides, it would seem impossible to know the truth of the matter. Far from being a handicap, I cannot but think this augments the power of the leader, thus endowed with the spectral glow that shines forth from the ambiguity of the ghost or ghost-to-be. All leaders are in effect transcendental beings, suspended between life and death. But in the current situation of Marulanda, neither dead nor alive, exemplar of liminality, this transcendence is magnified. As I write, Fidel Castro and Hugo Chávez are in much the same liminal state, hovering between life and death.

So let us pause for a moment to consider this curious *space of death*. For is it not death that provides the charmed space inhabited by Chupeta, by Marulanda, and by Fidel, and is not this same space the womb in which nicknames gestate? Site of rebirth, this space is quite literally a space of death, given that violence and the threat of death enshroud these folk. They dish death out and fear it as well. All the more suprising and wonderful that, as with gallows humor, tenderness and humor play around the nicknames they bear. In the case of cosmic surgery, the space of death prefiguring a rebirth of Self is obvious enough, most especially in the morbid stories of grotesque failures and death as a result of such surgery.

More mundane, perhaps, but also more widespread, are the opportunities for nicknaming implicit in choosing e-mail IDs and "user names." The feared upstate New York building inspector who wants permission to pack a gun on the job responds to "codeman," a lovable trapper in camouflage uses "pdogsoldier," while my old friend L. has chosen the unforgetable "headinavat."

Ordinary Names

But of course in Colombia, if not in other Latin American countries, nothing compares with the beauty of the real names bestowed by one's family. I have already mentioned the high-ranking Colombian guerrilla Juvenal Ovidio Ricardo Palmera Pineda, who had to paper over his wonderful real name with the utterly boring Simón

Trinidad, but let me proceed to the name bestowed by my friend Anabeba, aged around forty-five, who lives in the countryside south of Cali. She called her daughter Crazy, that is, Crazy Elvira Balanta Carabali.

On the way into town from Crazy's place there is a talented young woman of serious demeanor who runs an Internet café. Her face and shoulders are lacerated from a motorbike accident. Her name—her *real* name—is Emperatriz, which means Empress.

My young helper, who keeps close to me because his now-dead dad and I hung out a lot in the 1990s, is called Davison, after the Harley Davidson motorbikes. His uncle died three years ago, when a condom full of cocaine exploded in his stomach. The body stayed warm a long time.

And let us not forget that icon of icons, Simón Bolívar, whose full name was Simón José Antonio de la Santísima Trinidad Bolívar Palacios y Blanco.

Crazy.

Emperatriz.

Davison.

Simón José Antonio de la Santísima Trinidad Bolívar Palacios y Blanco.

By comparison, aliases are plain dull. Consider again Simón Trinidad, that brutal foreshortening of Bolívar's name chosen by the banker who lit off for the hills. You can hear the entire edifice of language groaning at the insult. Indeed, even nicknames—at least the ones I have mentioned—conform to a stripped-down shorthand: El Alemán (the German), Cuchillo (the Knife), and so on. Nevertheless, they partake of the magic of doubling and enlarge the theatricality of our world.

For nicknaming estranges names and naming. It causes us to look at names in a more conscious way, as more theatrical, not to be taken for granted. Seen thus, names are more like labels stuck onto and peeled off of persons, suggestive of forms of life lived doubly. Nicknames project their bearers onto the stage, where they become characters in a play—a Brechtian performance showing showing, replete with alienation effects—two-dimensional cutouts more surreal than real, more supernatural than natural.

The parallel with cosmic surgery is illuminating.

Nicknames and Cosmic Surgery

You can think of it like this. A nickname sits between one's real name and a false name, and it is in that ambiguous space also that I would place the face or body changed by cosmic surgery. To the extent that such a face or body is like a *false name* or an *alias*, it can seem inauthentic, strange, and troubling, and this is what we find in expressions of distaste toward cosmic surgery outside of Latino cultures, for example. On the other hand, you can, as I have been at pains to point out, think of a *nickname* not as false but as an adornment—like pearl earrings or a modish hat—and problems such as inauthenticity, being true to one's body, one's age, or one's looks, are irrelevant, which is precisely the aesthetic of the baroque, in which the love of the theatrical, the artificial, and the extravagant was second only to the labyrinthine complexity of the state, the corruption of the bureaucracy, and the heavenly ordained power of the king. It is in this way, then, that the aesthetic of cosmic surgery is today infused with the current political setup, that extravaganza of false faces.

"All that is left is your name," Olivia Mostacilla told me with vehemence, expatiating on the lengths to which high-profile criminals such as Chupeta and the Grouper go to change their identity through cosmic surgery. It was a forceful summation. "All that is left is your name," she declaimed as the final thrust to a crescendo of sarcastic commentary mixed with wonder at the miracles of cosmic surgery. Here we are at this momentous stage in world history, where much if not most of what seems essential to the identity of a person—their appearance—can be changed. As if by magic, they become someone else. Ugly people become beautiful. Fat people become thin. Old people become young. Serial killers in bed with the state are endowed with the beatific smile of a saint. The "you" of before, the original "you" of flesh and blood, of a certain weight and curvature of body and face, has vanished like a puff of smoke except for that label attached to the wraith of your being, the label of your name—if you still have one.

law in a lawless land

For fashion was never anything other than the parody of the motley cadaver, provocation of death through the woman, and bitter colloquy with decay whispered between shrill bursts of mechanical laughter. That is fashion.

WALTER BENJAMIN[1]

THAT IS FASHION, ACCORDING TO A HYPERBOLIC NOTE the usually sedate Benjamin wrote to himself. Fashion really gets him going, fashion as an elaborate tangle of metaphor. Not *really* death? Surely, that's just a figure of speech. Not *really* decay? *Not really* the motley cadaver? For heaven's sake! Provocation of death through the woman! Please!

That was then. But now it's all come true, or true enough, at least in certain places, and probably more than you think. Of course fashion is objectified metaphor. Therein lies its charm no less than its power of attraction. And so it will remain. But that by no means precludes the metaphors becoming real and fashion and death forming an indissoluble twosome. "You go about it one way, and I another," says Fashion to Death.[2]

"It always returns," Pepe the tailor insisted. "It always returns." He saw law at work and cheered it on. His was the law of the circle, the eternal return.

"Drill!" he exclaimed, pointing with pride to a locked display case, from which he extracted a pair of chinos made recently in Ibague, Colombia—the type of wide pants with cuffs that men have been wearing for a century along with a felt hat, a belt, and a tucked-in shirt, an ensemble some call *el clasico*.

A block from the town center, Pepe's shop was a sober reminder of how things used to be and how things should be. It had the high ceilings of the old adobe and bamboo buildings, with a dark, tidy air, its woodwork riddled with tiny holes, testimony to years in this tropical climate. Suspended from the ceiling and packed along the high walls were bales of dark cloth used to make suits for men. In the center of the room stood a locked vitrine ten feet high showcasing a few shirts and pants. It was like an altar—an altar to Dignity and the Way It Used To Be. Yet despite the passing of time and fashion his business chugged along. He was always there, energetically at his sewing machine, with a laugh and a sharp comment about the current state of mankind. Even though he was long "out of fashion," there was steady demand for his "look," he explained, as the plantations and factories and businesses in the city demanded that aspiring office employees not wear jeans or sneakers. Thus he benefited from reaction, the reaction against fashion in the fashion war that defines the epoch. In 2010, walking three blocks further on from his shop, I was advised in no uncertain terms that it was unsafe to walk one step more, not even to the block just beyond where I had lived serenely for over a year in 1970 and where I had visited without much fear or apprehension up till two years ago. The "war zone" was expanding at a fast clip, and on the other side I doubt there were many buying clothes from Pepe.

But "even young men are giving up on low-riders," Pepe told me with satisfaction in 2009. Every month they creep up a fraction of an inch. Yet when I told him, on leaving, that I needed to come back and talk more about clothing, he went into another of his rants. "Clothing! Clothing! *Un*-clothing, that's what it is!"—referring to the dress of girls and young women. His anger gave the lie to his confidence that "it always returns." He was apoplectic about lawlessness—at least this form of lawlessness—as if it would open the floodgates to hell and revolution.

At the same time as I was talking with Pepe I was reading Flaubert's *Sentimental Education*, set in Paris in the revolutionary year of 1848, and came across this scene of a party in a respectable bourgeois home:

The room was full of women sitting next to one another on backless seats. Their long skirts, puffed out around them, looked like waves from which their waists projected, and their low-cut bodices revealed their breasts. Nearly all of them were holding a bunch of violets. The dull color of their gloves heightened the natural whiteness of their arms; fringes and flowers hung down over their shoulders, and sometimes, when one of them shivered, it seemed as if her gown was going to fall. But the respectability of their faces compensated for the daring of their dresses; several of them indeed wore expressions of almost animal calm, and this gathering of half-naked women suggested a scene in a harem; a cruder comparison came into the young man's mind.[3]

Discussing the permissiveness of the Renaissance in his book on magic and Eros, Ioan Couliano draws attention to the radical changes in women's fashion in the fourteenth century, when "the neckline was cut so low 'that it was possible to see half the beasts.' Isabella of Bavaria introduced 'deep-necked dresses' cut down to the navel. Sometimes the breasts are completely bare, the nipples decorated with rouge or rings of precious stones and even pierced to permit insertion of little gold chains."[4]

So I had to concede Pepe something. It looks like his law of eternal return has a lot of truth, even if the examples that came my way were the opposite of what he wanted, with the startling revelation of woman's body, noted by Couliano and recorded by Flaubert at a time of revolutionary uncertainty in the capital of the nineteenth century, now being repeated in our time. And yet I cannot quite believe that in Colombia, and in most of today's world, this frankness toward the naked or near-naked female body is merely part of a recurrent cycle. I believe this exposure is new and fresh in Colombia, as in the rest of what is now called global south, ever since European colonization and especially since the missionaries got to work insisting on the shame of nakedness. Now, you know that a sexual revolution is occurring when you see an entire shelf in the bookstore in the Cali airport displaying books such as *Kama Sutra for Lesbians*, unthinkable five years before.

"Fashion has a flair for the topical, no matter where it stirs in the thickets of long ago; it is a tiger's leap into the past," wrote Benjamin in his "Theses on the Philosophy of History," and Pepe would nod in agreement at this curious surge backward into the future. Benjamin went on to draw a sharp contrast, however, between the "tiger's leap into the past" that is manipulated by the ruling class, and the tiger's leap "into the open air of history," which he sees as "dialectical" and as how "Marx understood the revolution." Well, the tiger is sure leaping now, and angry people like Pepe are actually not so sure as to its destination. Witness his locked vitrine with its classic styles of men's clothes, more an altar than a showcase of commodities. There is a dimly sensed awareness that although, as Bataille would have it, transgression enforces the taboo, this time around transgression for the sake of transgression shall proceed unabated "in the open air of history," where the tension between the rule and breaking the rule is what animate the tiger. What Hakim Bey calls "the temporary autonomous zone" may here not be all that temporary or all that pleasant.[5]

Teddy Adorno tore strips off Benjamin's 1935 grant proposal for what became, belatedly, the set of notes called *The Arcades Project.* The guiding light for this project was admittedly strange. It encompassed what Benjamin called an "awakening" from the dream sleep that capitalism had laid over Europe. This awakening was to be accomplished by nourishing the wish-images of utopia that are engendered by the interaction of old and new modes of economic production. And here we might envision Pepe's town, caught midway between a dying peasant agriculture and a zombied-out, factory-in-the-field mode of producton based on chemicals, machines, and a monopoly on land and water, together with a mass of unemployed and unemployable kids whose eyes are cast anywhere but toward working on the land or in a factory.

More than technology, it is to the stymied promises of technology that history moves. You see the new power, and you wonder, Why that? Why not . . . this? Meanwhile, homespun technology gets to work smuggling cocaine produced in ingeniously homemade laboratories hidden in the mountains nearby. At the same time, the old-timers lovingly recall the golden age of the peasant garden, like that other garden we call, following the Arabs, paradise.

It was to the impact of the stymied promise of technology that Benjamin directed attention. The mix of old and new in the early nineteenth century spawned science-fiction fantasies such as those dreamed up by the utopian socialists Charles Fourier and Saint-Simon, who urged radical economic and sociocultural changes to family arrangements and sexuality in accord with the fairy-tale promise latent in the technology of the industrial revolution. Grafted onto myths and fantasies stirring in the collective consciousness, technology could thus be rerouted so as to usher in lands of milk and honey that would resonate with a golden age of classlessnes, as in the saying associated with John Ball and the peasants' uprising of 1381, "When Adam delved and Eve span, who was then the gentleman?"

What annoyed Benjamin's philosopher friend, Teddy Adorno, about these tumultuous ideas was that they appeared too one-sided in favor of utopia. What about hell? he asked. What about catastrophe and a foreboding sense of alienation? Doesn't that appear in the phantasmagoria of the early industrial revolution in Europe too? It was an interesting criticism, given that of all people Benjamin would surely be the first to pin catastrophe on the chest of history, as evidenced by his panic-stricken Angel of History with its back to the future, struggling to fly forward, which in this case meant back in time, into paradise, from where a fierce wind called "progress" makes it impossible to make much headway. I think Pepe would understand, as he regretfully, yet with considerable pride, puts *el clasico* back into the locked display case and warns me emphatically against walking more than two blocks east, where Eve spins ever more revealing garments and Adam delves ever deeper in the lands of derring-do.

If I look farther afield than Pepe's shop, to the remote gold mining village of Santa María de Timbiquí on the trackless Pacific coast of Colombia, there is an old, old tailor-man, his long, bony legs battered by falling rocks over many decades spent working as a miner in the fast-flowing Cesé River. His name is Gustavo Cesbén and he is not only a miner. With his foot-pedal Singer sewing machine he can still make men's shirts and women's dresses, and he is outraged by contemporary women's fashion. "It shows everything!" he shrieks, and he bends down close to the ground to show me how long women's dresses used to be.

Consider his sewing machine, a machine for making wonders, as when he makes exquisite bedspreads from scraps of old clothes—old blue jeans, old shirts, old skirts, and old blouses, tatters and shreds torn adrift by years of work by villagers braced in the fast flowing water of the river or the mud and boulders of the mines. I bought a bedspread from him. You would be hard put to find anything like it elsewhere, with its rough seams, fabulous colors, and formal arrangement of blocks of solid color and patterned fabrics—purples, shiny grays, yellows, dark blue polka dots on a light blue background, and a marvelous faint yellow panel with pink and yellow flowers placed just off center. He spreads it out in front of him while sitting barefoot by his sewing machine. Like a great flower it billows, then settles on the cement floor. This is the flowering of history, shreds of the work-

worn, patched and repatched past "renovated" in a billowing field of beauty that intimates the utopia to which Benjamin alludes, no less than the hell Adorno said was fast on its heels.

Here in Santa María, lost in the misty headwaters of one of the world's more isolated rivers, the school prohibits boys from wearing earrings or low-riding pants and requires that they tuck in their shirts, although these restrictions, like most local rules, are enforced by gossip and custom, rarely by force, which, when it occurs, can be bloody indeed. What skin girls may expose is likewise regulated.

Yet outside of school the kids do their thing, and the distance to the great centers of corruption—the large cities in the interior—daily grows less. In fact, there is a veritable hotline to the interior as kids on the lam for murder or worse claim some family connection and sneak back to hide in their villages amid the jungle. There are even a couple of the frightening paramilitaries known as the Black Eagles hiding out in this village, young hipsters sporting the latest haircuts, clothes, and accessories, although they never look you in the eye. How strange they are, trying to look chill, sauntering down the one street this village has, lined by two-story wooden houses strung along the edge of the fast-flowing river. They carry a lot of aura, that's for sure, a mix of braggadocio and evil, an aura like black exhaust blowing in the winds of history. People are frightened by them. How strange that one of the beacons of fashion in this remote jungle town should be these professional killers. Or could it be they are just sweet innocent boys whom, because they dress the way they do, have been miscategorized as paid assassins?

Fashion may have obeyed the law of eternal return in the past. Transgression may only have suspended the taboo, not broken it. But now those days look pathetically innocent, as transgression forges effervescent spin cycles around the taboo. "We are the first generation," wrote the historian Eric Hobsbawm in 2002, on turning eighty-five, "to have lived through the historic movement when the rules and conventions that hitherto bound human beings together in families, communities and societies ceased to operate. If you want to know what it was like, only we can tell you. If you think you can go back, we can tell you, it can't be done."[6] This is why Pepe and Gustavo Cesbén are shrieking even though they are a long way from Hobsbawm's London (which is part of his point).

So much for history. So much for change. The old historian with his wealth of experience and seasoned judgments earmarks the change and its intensity. We can call it different things, such as the rebellion of the young, and see in that the age-old story of bellicose youth, a revolt that seems more properly peculiar to our age. But now, is there not another world forming around the young, something new in world history?

When I think back to how the body—especially the young female body—was presented in rural Colombia in the 1970s and 80s, the change today is beyond radical. What has happened in merely the past ten years is overwhelming. And this particular shift is merely one of the changes challenging not just previous clothing and aesthetic norms but the very nature of authority. Che Guevara once prophesied a New Man. Well, here she is.

Indeed, we could go further, as with Zygmunt Bauman's distinction between the "modern" body of the soldier/producer and that of the "postmodern" consumer, the former evaluated in terms of its regimented capacity to work and fight, the latter, its capacity to consume, which means, he says, "the ability to be aroused, a finely tuned sensitivity to pleasurable stimuli, readiness to absorb new sensations and openness to new, untested and therefore exciting experience." This body is an instrument of pleasure, and unlike the body of the producer, which is regulated by rules, this is a "norm-defying and norm-transcending" body.[7]

Bauman wants to bring up another momentous contrast here with his suggestion that, as regards the body, a certain symbiosis between death and religion gives way to a cult of health and medicine. But among the poor of the third world, don't things take a different turn? The "postmodern body" morphs into the freeing up of death combined with the cult of cosmic surgery. Death now stalks the streets as a spectator sport. Life is not so much cheap as virtual, like the bodies of the liposucked.

Setting the terms for my history of beauty as a history of norm-defiance and norm- transcendence (hence Beauty *and* the Beast), the art of fashion comes across strikingly in the names of the gangs such as Los Sin Futuros and the Dandies. A new way of being is born as much for the "people who have no future" as for the Dandies—a name connoting a way of walking, a way with guns, a way of styling your hair, a way of music, a way with girls, a way of taking someone down for a few dollars, a pair of sneakers, a bicycle, a mobile phone, or a motorbike. The coexistence of dandyism with an ironic acceptance of the end of the world—Los Sin Futuros—speaks to fashion as a new way of life oriented toward death, a life replete with fragmentation grenades, off-the-charts homicide rates, and a most complete and thoroughgoing rejection of the way of the fathers, a refusal to conform to what society used to be about.

"Fashion is the death ritual of the commodity," wrote Walter Benjamin. That was in western Europe in the 1930s. Fast forward to the third world today, where death has become the ritual of fashion. Not for these kids what their landless parents did uncomplainingly, standing in the heat and rain digging ditches for the sugar plantations, cutting cane, or being a live-in servant in the city with half a day off every two weeks. And here's the point: weren't these gangs of incomprehensible youth—responsible for some 80 percent of all homicides in Colombia, including deaths at the hands of the guerrilla, the army, and the paramilitaries—weren't these gangs doing exactly the same as what was being enacted on the nature around them by machines and chemicals? That's a fashion too. That's a death ritual too. With its own aesthetic.

Over it all hangs the promise of the apocalypse, the coming of the end. *We have no future.* Evangelical temples sprout like mushrooms. People sway and wail, dressed in their Sunday best every day of the week. They pay 10 percent of their income to greedy pastors and live with their heads in the future world, waiting for their bodies to follow. So they sway and wail and shuffle to the next funeral of some young relative gunned down by some other young relative. And really, they don't have to wait for the end. It is going on all around them, in the mad sexual beauty of fashion and in the destruction of the surrounding land and its people.

Beauty and the Beast walk hand in hand. One implies the other. There is no other way. Sex and the glories and mysteries of the underworld surface stronger and stranger each day. Death and the underworld has its own fashion runway, as seen in the burials of gangsters by their fellow gang members. There they stand, high on the walls of the cemetery, flouting the taboos surrounding the dead even as they pay homage to death itself. For all the world they resemble the buzzards hunched shoulder to shoulder on the crumbling brick walls of the abattoir six blocks away by the river, once a joyous waterway.

Once upon a time the cemetery fed the church, providing it with the sacred energy of the corpse, which the church converted into its sacred power, while the abattoir in the center of the town, where the buzzards perch, was set apart from this circuit, remaining encased in its putrid bubble by the river. But now with the new dispensation it seems that the "negative sacred" of the abattoir displaces the siphoning off of souls by the church and that it is this that comes to define the new sacred power astir in today's world. What, more exactly, is this new sacred? Why, it is transgression itself, the new god after the death of god. New angels—fallen angels—now perch on the walls of the cemetery and with rap music and *reggaeton* way loud, the Dandies and Los Sin Futuros invent new rites of death.

The crowd bunched outside the cemetery is fearful. It is all so thrilling. But what is the attraction in the repulsion? The crowd sways back and forth. Rumors fly of an imminent shootout. By whom? For what? It's crazy. We are drawn in by the incomprehensibility of it all. Panic seizes the crowd at the slightest sign, moving to the left, then to the right, like a school of fish pursued by phantom shadows across the shallows. Last time I got close, the police, not the gangsters, were standing on the walls, shoulder to shoulder like the vultures they are.

An airliner passed overhead. Later that week, August 12, 2007, I saw a photograph in *El Tiempo* showing a young woman in bra and panties, hands nonchalantly on her hips, flowing black hair tossed behind her cocked head, lips pursed, chin out—standing in the aisle of a regularly scheduled airliner flying at thirty thousand feet between Quito and Guayaquil. Two middle-aged men, eyes magnified by their glasses, stand erect in their seats, transfixed, while a younger one remains seated with a look of incredulity. It was reported there were several such women on this aerial catwalk, displaying the designs of Leonisa, an Ecuadorian fashion house, taking fashion to the skies.

Could the history of beauty I am tracing lie in this concatenation of flight with death, of seminaked goddesses displaying fashion high above the meticulously dressed girls and boys of the criminal underworld busy in the graveyard? As befits our modern era given over to cosmic surgery, I am catapulted into an ancient cosmic

Diario el Comercio (Quito, Ecuador).

scheme—a veritable shamanic flight through the heavens, scaling the *axis mundi* so beloved by our shamanologists. Only in this case what I find is a norm-transcendent female body in the air connected thus to the corpses of the gangstas, where underground meets underground, where the ground of the cemetery filling with sewage water meets the undergound of the law, while the living stand guard in their finery. A bizarre suggestion, no doubt, this idea of shamanic flight in the heavens and under the ground, like what used to happen in those far-off days when shamans knew a thing or two and saw beauty in the body opening up resplendent with color and flowers and wonderful scents.[8] And I think of droll Raúl in the cemetery with his story of the septuagenerian pepped up on Viagra, dying in erotic spasm, and of the swaths of young men similarly pepped, raring to go but ending up here with *regatón* singing them to sleep forever. I think of Dionysus, half god, half man, half woman too, some thought, perceived as both man and animal, capable of great violence and of dance, drugged out, locked in the trance of divine madness, theater, impersonation, and mimesis—and no stranger to the rites and myths of the mysterious realm of the dead.[9] I think of Nima's beautifying salon a few blocks south. How close it is, this magic of beauty she makes possible. How close it is to the sorcery that the bones and dirt of the cemetery provide. A history of beauty. Why does it seem strange?

the tabooed cleft

I WANTED TO LEARN MORE about the technique of liposuction and went to the cosmic surgery department of the main public hospital in Cali where selective liposuction was carried out, supposedly for medical, not cosmetic, reasons. After a good deal of searching by an assistant, the surgeon was able to show me a sterilized blue and white cloth bundle containing five cannulas used in a typical *lipo*, hefty metal tubes about eighteen inches long with a good grip at one end and holes at the other. On the floor was a stainless steel vacuum pump and a glass bottle into which the fat and blood sucked from the body via the cannula would make its way. The surgeon told me liposuction began in France with the aim of sculpting the body.

I had heard this phrase—*sculpting the body*—a few times, and I must say it affected me. If Botox to eliminate wrinkles or cosmic surgery on the nose and one's smile represent a significant intrusion into nature, then how much more of an intrusion, how much more cosmic, is sculpting the body?

The words make me think not only of the Creator with his clay but also, for some reason, of ice sculpture. Perhaps this is because ice, unlike malleable clay, is clean and pure and hard, yet brittle and passive before the sculptor's pick. Perhaps I discern the same force, if not aggression, in the manipulation of the cosmic surgeon's scalpel as in the blows delivered by the sculptor's chisel? What is more, like something in a fairy tale, an ice sculpture is destined for a tragically short life—which makes it all the more miraculous and beautiful, like Bataille's flowers doomed to wither into refuse after their moment of glory. An ice sculpture melts at temperatures to which humans are accustomed. Like cosmic surgery, it cannot last.

And as in a fairy tale, this original, French procedure of liposuction, the surgeon went on to tell me, was brought to an abrupt halt for several decades after the death of a famous ballerina, whose arteries were severed by the sharp edge of the cannula. So I didn't have to go out looking for beauty's beast. It was right there at the beginning of the story. Otherwise I was disoriented. Finding my way to the heartland of *lipo* on the second floor of the hospital, I was several times lost. On the way in, I had wandered around piles of rubble in the courtyard and been surprised by a man wearing a gauze mask and wheeling a corpse on a gurney, its face covered but its bare feet protruding. Later I wondered if those bare feet weren't preparing me for the sad tale of the ballerina. It also struck me that covering the face of the body was not only a sign of respect for the dead but also an acknowledgment of the mystical importance of the face during life that death illuminates.

So much for the sanctity of the face, that playground for cosmic surgery. But then there is fat, loved and hated in equal measure and no less sacred than the human face. Neither sexual nor soulful, at least not in any direct way, fat is nevertheless most definitely charged with the metaphysical and the magical. We cannot think of the human face, it seems to me, without also considering human fat. Face and fat go together in the larger scheme of things. And fat even more than face lends itself to the fairy tale, nowhere more so than in stories of fat from liposuction being sold for magical purposes. One callow artist in Switzerland has gone so far as to claim a block of soap he has made will wash away corruption. On sale for US $18,000 a block (at 2005 prices), it is called *Clean Hands* and was made from the fat sucked out of Italy's prime minister, Silvio Berlusconi—a fine figure of a man, and now we know why.[1]

Jon Carter, who lived for over two years in Honduras, tells me that in 2005 he several times heard from poor urban people there that fat from liposuction, a procedure then available only to the well-to-do, was used to make expensive face creams. Digging deeper, he showed me a clip from the 1999 movie *Fight Club,* in which the central characters steal human fat from the dumpster of a liposuction clinic so as to make fancy soap and hence big money, selling to the rich "what came from their fat arses." One of the thieves adds that the glycerin from human fat is so fine that it can be used to make dynamite by adding nitric acid.

Consider also the stories about *Nakaq*, who puts Indians in the Peruvian Andes to sleep and extracts fat from them so as to make medicines, grease machinery, cast church bells, and shine the faces of the saints. As a consequence the victim slowly dies or falls into prolonged depression.

Could there be history at work here? Consider that at the core of the greatest Andean Indian revolt against the Spanish was the story that the Spanish were amassing Indian body fat to export to Spain to make medicines for the people there. That was the Dance Sickness uprising, or Taqui Onqoy, in the mid-sixteenth century.

Not only Indians have weird beliefs about Europeans and their desire for fat. One of Cortés's lieutenant's, the famous chronicler Bernal Díaz, tells how the Spanish soldiers in the conquest of Mexico would use Indian fat to heal their wounds as well of those of their horses.

Taking your enemy's kidney fat by mystical or by physical means was a cause of great concern to indigenous people in the Daly River area of Northern Australia in the 1930s. In an incident discussed by the anthropologist W. E. H. Stanner, an indigenous man publicly declared that he had seen an incision in his nephew's side and that the murderer had a tin containing human fat and red ocher. Stanner explains: People were "actually cut open for their fat, which was thought to have life-giving and protective properties."[2] Note the "actually."

Can we discern here different fat registers: premodern, modern, even postmodern? What the Spaniards wanted, and what the Nakaq wants, is a substance deemed so critical to a person's essence that removal is fatal or at least soul-depleting, while by the same token it is life-enabling for those who receive it. By contrast, modern fat is less overtly magical and hovers in the West between the sexually attractive (in Rubenesque "Venus at the Mirror" women) and the jovial male ectomorph who inhabited scientific psychology well into the twentieth century, while postmodern fat swings 180 degrees to become magical in a quite different way, that of the abject and the repulsive, the definition of what one should *not* be. As for the ex-colonies, I heard a Nigerian novelist say recently that what struck her most on coming to live in the United States, what was truly strange, was that in Nigeria the rich were fat and the poor thin, while in the USA it was the other way around.

Whatever the period or place, then, fat comes across as a highly charged substance, which is why it appears to such startling effect in the artwork of Joseph Beuys, one of the most original artists of the twentieth century. A mystical, even shamanic, artist to some, an essentializing, even fascistic, figure to others, a radical environmentalist and pro-working class, pro-student democrat to still others, his fat throws the critics into a frenzy of conflicting evaluations. Such is fat.

A poignant indicator of the highly charged ambiguity of fat is the impressive contrast today when hitherto unimagined levels of obesity exist side by side with cocaine-induced, anorexic thinness as fact and ideal.

Gulliver's Travels needs a new chapter.

Small wonder that as I walked out of the hospital after my visit to the liposuction clinic, I saw fat everywhere. Fat has such a rich mythology and what I had witnessed in the clinic, with its gleaming glass and stainless steel pumps sucking out fat, was no more that a blip in a far older story. And let's not forget the cannulas—how I've come to love that word—wrapped tenderly in their blue and white cloths. My life had been changed. Now I was like some supermodel supersensitive to the regnant adiposity.

All around me were young and not so young women wearing blouses cut short of their midriff, exposing the navel and the muffin of fat bulging over the tops of tight, low-cut jeans—definitely candidates for *lipo*. And when they bent over or squatted, the tabooed cleft in the buttocks burst upon the scene, often elaborated by a tattoo of a flower or cosmic design.

Butt cleavage is how I heard the tabooed cleft referred to in 2008 on the radio in New York City. The voluble writer being inteviewed about pulp fiction was asked about the racy covers of his books and responded that covers were racier in the 1950s. Then it was possible to have a picture of a nude woman on the book jacket—but not now. No way! he said, because now books must be sold through Wal-Mart and other megastores, which, determined to protect the decency of the American consumer, do not allow such lewdness. Wal-Mart had made him pull a jacket recently because it showed too much butt cleavage. The woman interviewing him giggled at the term, and he admitted that this had been the first time he had heard it. Imagine! A Wal-Mart invention, or at least a neologism. All of which goes to show that the taboo is still very much intact, even though fashion butts against it.

I recall the mechanic up the road from where I live in upstate New York, a rather obese fellow whose grease-stained pants subside to reveal a generous amount of the tabooed cleft whenever he leans over to peer into a car engine. As he invariably comes to the conclusion that the situation is hopeless and that you had better sell the car as soon as possible, it is not surprising that some young women I know refer to him (behind his back) as "the crack of doom." These women have certainly caught the poetry of the eternal, bringing to mind a point made about fashion in Paris in 1937 by none other than Roger Caillois; that the most trifling details of fashion are worth studying, as they can be easily turned into moral and philosophical questions.[3] But the young women upstate are more poetic.

When I first came to western Colombia in 1969 it was, as I recall, uncommon for women of any social class, urban or rural, to wear trousers except for work in the fields and farms. They most certainly did not not wear low-riders and would have been mortified at the thought of it. There was absolutely no way, materially or culturally, that the tabooed cleft could be bared. The world has become a smaller place since then, and low-riders have spread. But curiously, much of the transgressive tension remains the same. More female skin is exposed, so in that sense a taboo is broken. But is it really broken? Now the cleft is visible, depending on posture, but like the advanced breasts in the Cali airport, it is as much unseen as seen.

How might one even begin to "explain" this scotomic vision, this seeing and not seeing at the same time? Freud had his fantasy of the mother's nonexistent phallus that is actively (not) seen by the little boy, but surely this is merely one instance of a more general phenomenon entailed by transgression? After all, what could be more transgressive than this young chap stealing (as we say) a glance, whether by accident or by design, bringing to mind those other founding figures of transgression, namely Adam and Eve in the Garden of Eden, reaching out for the fruit of the tree of good and evil and ending up with a fig leaf?

For is it not the case that it is at the moment of transgression that you see-and-don't-see, thus entering into a topsy-turvy world of ambiguities and wild imaginings? In the case of Genesis, these imaginings take the form of a good story, good enough to sustain the origin of good and evil apportioned into its male and female components. According to psychoanalysis, it is vision itself that is subject to wild imaginings once the taboo has been transgressed and we are cast into the wilderness, creating a space out of time charged with mythologies, conflict, excitement, and fear—to such a degree that a high-energy, undulating wave perturbs normality. This, then, is transgression, this instability, this kick given to reality, like the "marvelous" in Surrealism, counterpart to the myths regnant in previous epochs now somersaulting into modernity, as with that glow espied by Louis Aragon in a dingy Paris arcade: "A glaucous gleam seemingly filtered through deep water, with the special quality of pale brilliance of a leg suddenly revealed under a lifted skirt."[4]

In seeing the tabooed cleft, one acknowledges the breaking of the rule. In actively not seeing it, one acknowledges the rule.

To this I should add the obvious point that fashion excites with its newness *because* it will soon become habitual and die. What is elided by the obviousness of this observation is the relish with which it is repeatedly pronounced as if it itself is fashionable and therefore about to die. There is something immensely satisfying in exulting the newness, yet even more in pronouncing its demise. The beauty and the beastliness of beauty lies in this whiplash effect, which parallels the logic of taboo and transgression made manifest by the visible invisibility of the tabooed cleft.

Benjamin expressed this in an inflammatory metaphor when he wrote that yesterday's fashion is not only anti-aphrodisiacal but radically so. The aphrodisiacal and anti-aphrodisiacal surges in fashion are dependent on the life-and-death rhythm of the fashion cycle, which, like the transgression of a taboo, creates an undulating wave along which we travel, suspended between yesterday and tomorrow, between the rule and breaking the rule. As we coast on the cutting edge of fashion, we bloom as social objects, both creative and created. If the father of sociology, Emile Durkheim, saw religion as society worshipping itself, then how much more does this apply to fashion, fashion being the fertile edge where being different but not too different is busy at work, undoing, redoing, and thereby fortifying the social contract. If we are neglectful of the short time span allotted the fashion, if we outlive the fashion, we lose our sheen and enter into that abysmal world Benjamin referred to as radically anti-aphrodisiac. It sounds terrible.

Thus the two waves constitutive of society mix and combine, one being the transgression and restoration of the taboo, the other being the waxing and waning of fashion's cycle.

Yet is this not too neat, more logical than sociological? Is there not something happening today that hampers the ability of the taboo to spring back after its transgression? Throughout the world, it seems, business as usual has been set aside, whether it be in fashion, Occupy Wall Street, or the Arab Spring. As the world teeters on the abyss of economic and environmental meltdown, society has entered into a state of suspension and the social contract is now very much a work in progress—a game inventing itself as it proceeds—such that what we might call "the taboo structure" no longer operates as it is meant to. This is more than anomie or normlessness. It is a state of permanent challenge and invention arising from the energy the taboo invests in its transgression, creating an out-of-body experience in which human bodies metamorphose into other sorts of bodies and other states of being and nonbeing.

There is an extraordinarily interesting tension in this state of suspension of the norm. For it can unleash the creation of new desires, new fashions, and new ways of being human. As such it is the wellspring of anarchism reaching out for a more just world combined with continuous experimentation with ways of being. By the same token, however, it can summon up all that is terrifying about modernity with regard to new forms of economic production, smashing tradition along with people and the environment. This is certainly what has happened in a remarkably short period of time to the landscape around my town, that "body of the world," and this is how I think of the tabooed cleft with reference to Benjamin's suggestion—surreal, to be sure, marvelous, to be sure—that fashion transports us as if on a spiritual journey into the world of inanimate things and substances—very much including, I would say, the human body because, as the privileged zone of taboo, the body so wonderfully sets off culture from nature while combing them in that mad vortex where human and natural history perturb each other's being.

At one point in his musings on the female body and fashion, Benjamin suggests that the erotic element tied to death may be manifest in what are seen as dreamy landscapes of the female body. Such landscapes are not unknown to anthropology, albeit with the balance swung not to death but to life and the cosmic significance of transgression. For instance, Max Guckman writes of a certain Zulu goddess, described to him in the mid-twentieth century by tribespeople in southern Africa as being dressed with light, who came from heaven to teach people how to make beer, how to plant, and how to carry out the useful arts. Every spring she returns, this goddess, clothed in light. When you look at her she appears as a beautiful landscape with verdant forests on some parts of her body, grass-covered slopes on other parts, and cultivated slopes elsewhere. When she returns like this, taboos are broken by humans. It is not that they *may* be broken but that they *have to* be broken. Girls dress like men, whose weapons they carry. They drive and milk cattle, activities that are at other times taboo to women. At times they strip naked. Men and boys become frightened and hide.[5]

Neither a capitalist nor a market-oriented society, and in most senses of the word not a "fashion-centered" one, this Zulu world as described by Gluckman "womanizes" the landscape, thanks to a goddess dressed in light, as prelude to the rites of spring. Now nature stirs into life. A jolt of transgression tears through the cosmos as women become men and real men disappear in fear. Yet this transgression has its limits, thereby ensuring spring no less than the eternal return.

But with Benjamin's evocation of fashion as the wheel of the capitalist economy and its ethos, not life but life-in-death is what guides the dream image of woman as landscape, landscape as woman. Witness Benjamin's remarks on fashion, which I cited earlier: "For fashion was never anything other than the parody of the motley cadaver, provocation of death through the woman."[6] This suggests a way of thinking about the photograph of women weeding in the cane fields (see page 87). Foreground: women in white clothes that are not clothes at all, but shrouds. Many women. At all angles, like pickets holding down the earth, holding up the sky. Out of balance. Out of balance with history. Background: the darkness behind, the dying farms of the peasant. Back to the women emergent in white from those farms. Benjamin has his own mythology to pursue, a sort of mirror image of the Zulu spring, a fantasy in which the dream image of landscape as woman is guided through the valley of death, giving rise to "swelling breasts, that like the earth, are all appareled in woods and rocks, and gazes have sent their life to the bottom of glassy lakes that slumber in valleys." Fashion, he asserts, drives such a gaze "still deeper into the universe of matter."[7] Is this what happens with the gaze into the tabooed cleft, driven still deeper into the universe of matter?

the fat kid
and the devil

CONSUMED BY IMAGES OF THE DEAD BALLERINA, the corpse on
the gurney, and the magisterial calm of the surgeon in the liposuction clinic with his cannulas wrapped tender as babies, I mounted
the bus to the impoverished town where I was living. A fat young
man, about fifteen, lounging in expensive clothes, sat next to the
driver, both he and the driver pawing the ticket collector, a nubile
girl squeezed between them, a roll of belly fat exposed. In my forty
years of catching this bus I can't recall having seen a fat young man
like this, the picture of indolence. Nor have I seen a female ticket
collector, let alone one with rolls of belly exposed. My thoughts flew
to the razor-thin cane cutters creating the non-cocaine wealth of
this land, then to my photographer friend in Aguablanca, a walking
corpse with hooded eyes and taut lips pulled back from his teeth, as
if all they wanted was to lunge at a steak.

When the bus pulled into the dusty town, I stopped at the herbal
medicine stall of Antonio Benavides. Putumayo herbalists like him
from the upper Amazon are as famous for their magic as for their
botany. Indeed, it would be a mistake to separate the two. In the
ten minutes we chatted, two women came by. The first had a huge
body, especially her backside. The second seemed in a higher economic stratum, not as fat but still obese by my reckoning. Both
wanted something I had never before heard of: herbs to lose weight.

Mr. Benavides claimed he had just the thing, a *jarabe* to *adelgarse*, but he refused to tell me, his friend of thirty years, what it contained. Such an herb is a novelty in his pharmacopoeia, largely derived from fantastic zones like the far-off rain forests of the Amazon, the Pacific coast, and Blessed Isles that noone but him has heard of. Yet this new *jarabe* certainly suits the current situation. Not as manifestly dramatic, perhaps, as *la lipo*, with its cannulas and the body corsets that bulk out the mummies in the back of Alberto's cab, but no less mythic.

Back in the 1970s when you met a peasant around the small town in which I lived, in the south of Colombia's Cauca Valley, you would go through elaborate formalities of greeting. Occasionally the ethnographer would have his or her calf gently massaged, being felt for fat, considered a sign of good health—and maybe a sign of something more, that promise of good fortune brought to those upon whom the gods smile. And if they were lucky enough themselves to be more than muscle and bone, these Afro-Colombians bore their weight with grace on their broad shoulders and long limbs. Fat in those days was an unmistakable sign of bounty, and fat was good. At the same time, fat was sure to make others envious, so watch out as that hand caresses your plump calf and you hear the purring voice of admiration, because envy is the root of sorcery.

But at least there and then we have a person. Shadowy he or she may be, the rarely named person doing the alleged sorcerery, at once alarming and unreal. But how much more real was that anonymous shadow compared to the anonymous force of fashion we confront today, let alone the new type of envy we feel toward the Other, thin and beautiful? Hence women mummify themselves and, thanks to cosmic surgery, become playthings of the gods.

Yet sorcery too has its fashions. Sorcery too changes with changes in the economy and ways of life. Could it be otherwise? In the legendary devil contract made famous by Faust, a person achieved short-lived magical benefits followed by consequences too horrible to imagine. The devil contracts I heard about in the agribusiness cane fields of the southern Cauca Valley in 1972 had some of this too, although with a melodrama. Here the story was that a cane cutter could more than double his wage through such a contract, but this would prevent sugarcane from growing in that area thereafter, and the money gained could be used only for luxury consumption, such as butter and dark glasses—not for food for one's children, for example. Nor could the money be used to rent a plot of land or buy an animal, such as a pig, to fatten for market. As with the land where the sugarcane was being cut, a rented plot of land would become infertile and livestock would die.

On the other hand, women were rarely if ever said to make such devil contracts, and upon questioning, it seemed that there was a logic at work here. "Is it not the women who are responsible for raising children?" So what good would the devil's wages serve? The few remaining local peasant farmers, with their small plots adjoining the ever-expanding planations, were like the women in that they were never mentioned as parties to devil contracts. Why would they want to render their farms sterile by doing that?

It seems possible that no devil contract was ever actually transacted. I think some were, but rarely. More important, however, is the story, which at that time many people believed or wanted to believe, and which they acted out with great energy when telling it. It is a story endowed with enough credibility that even if it is only a story taken for real, that by no means diminishes its power, which touches the deepest layers of morality and economy—including the nature of growth, whether plant, animal, or human, whether in the peasant economy, the modern capitalist economy of the field as factory, or, now, the magical economy of the body and beauty.

Could it be that today—forty years after I first heard of the devil contract—that this fairy tale of the devil lives on, not so much in the cane fields, where it appears to have died out, but applied now to women and society's demand for beautification and glamor? For do not my stories of *la lipo* and cosmic surgery resonate perfectly with the story of the contract with the devil? What could be more cosmic?

Each of these stories, of men in the cane fields and women undergoing cosmic surgery, draws its power from a wondrous technological referent that recedes ever deeper into mystery and magic. With the cane cutters, we have the devil contract, which increases wages but renders nature barren. With the women undergoing surgery, nobody talks of the devil per se, but he is surely present, insofar as the promise of beauty is dashed on the rocks of disaster. He is present in the medley of glamor and disfiguration. He is there in Alberto's yellow cab, smiling, riding home side by side with the mummy corseted in bandages. Sometimes he is his handsome, devilish self, like Chupeta, who could stand in for a 1950s hair-cream advertisement—before his face was changed surgically, becoming progressively more misshapen and hideous. Other days the devil is remorseful, his hands in an attitude of prayer, like the paramilitary chieftan Salvatore Mancuso with his "confession" and designer smile. And still other days he is a rattling bag of bones with empty eye sockets and a fixed grin, the skeleton of El Mexicano, José Gonzalo Rodríguez Gacha, he of the gold-embossed toilet paper. These men of the underworld are gods whose directive is not to make the world in seven days but to dominate it, first and foremost through the body of woman, 90-60-90. There they sit in Armenia in the foothills of the lush *cordillera central*, those lazy warm afternoons, sipping cold beer, watching mothers parade their young daughters, in Armenia and everywhere else, including the lands of the imagination.

The distinction between magic and technology, surrealism and realism, becomes blurred because the stories deal with epoch-breaking moments in the history of the body—on the one hand, the body of the earth as transformed by agribusiness; on the other hand, the body of woman as transformed by the revolution in capitalism from production-focus to consumption-focus, from taboo to transgression. History proceeds not in smooth, evolutionary steps but in ruptures—figured by earthquakes and exploding breasts—and by these moments of mythology to host the sense of the marvelous.

This change in focus, from the labor of men working in modern agribusiness to the beautification of women, resonates with the turn the world over from the heroic task of production to the heroism of individual consumption, the revealed-and-concealed female body being the center of desire around which consumerism revolves. For the truth of the matter now is that all of us will plunge ahead, beautifying and buying regardless of the devil—indeed because of the devil dishing out his oh-so-enjoyable stories of horror in relation to liposculpture. Yes, the devil does wear Prada, and fashion taunts the taboo with ever more electrifying force as the realm of the aesthetic embraces bodily mutilations by paramilitaries alongside agribusiness mutilations of our Mother the earth. It is as if the pulse of taboo, bound to its law of attracting and then repelling transgression, has been fundamentally changed. In today's insatiable world the state of suspension between law and the breach of the law yawns ever wider. And into this gap pours *depense*, the extreme and beyond— like those eyes subjected to cosmic surgery and now unable to close. Imagine trying to sleep like that.

And she laughed.

THE END

acknowledgments

My seamstress friend of forty years, Olivia Mostacilla, resident of Puerto Tejada, Cauca, was the first to draw my attention to the singular importance of *la lipo* in recent years, and her insights into fashion fill out this book. With his droll humor and shrewd observations, Raúl Zuniga, also of Puerto Tejada, makes me continuously aware of what I am unaware. Nancy Goldring tried vainly to keep me on track regarding beauty, and my daughter Olivia Ambrosia supplied me with a precious drawing of D. H. Lawrence's grandfather's sewing machine as well as the cover image.

notes

Gift of the Gods

1 Paul Krugman, "Revenge of the Glut" (op-ed), *New York Times*, March 2, 2009, A23.

2 E. E. Evans-Pritchard, *Nuer Religion* (Oxford: Oxford University Press, 1956), 256–57, 279. Georges Bataille, "The Concept of Expenditure," in *Visions of Excess: Selected Writings, 1927–1939*, trans. and ed. Alan Stoekl (Minneapolis: University of Minnesota Press, 1985), 116–29. The term *toomuchness* I take from Norman O. Brown, "Dionysus in 1990," in *Apocalypse and/or Metamorphoses* (Berkeley: University of California Press, 1991).

3 Inga Clendinnen, "The Cost of Courage in Aztec Society," *Past and Present*, no. 107 (May 1985), 16–89. Henri Hubert and Marcel Mauss, *Sacrifice: Its Nature and Function* (1898; Chicago: University of Chicago Press, 1964), 22–25.

4 Bronislaw Malinowski, *Argonauts of the Western Pacific* (1922; Long Grove, IL: Waveland, 1984), 341.

5 Ibid., 239. E. E. Evans-Pritchard, *Witchcraft, Oracles, and Magic among the Azande* (Oxford: Clarendon Press, 1937).

6 Malinowski, *Argonauts*, 251.

7 Ibid., 339.

8 Walter Benjamin, "The Storyteller: Reflections on the Works of Nicolai Leskov," in *Illuminations*, ed. Hannah Arendt (New York: Schocken, 1968), 102.

9 Walter Benjamin, cited in Egon Wissing, "Protocol of the Experiment of March 7, 1931," in Benjamin, *On Hashish* (Cambridge, MA: Harvard University Press, 2006), 69.

10 Georges Bataille, *The Accursed Share: An Essay on General Economy*, vol. 1, *Consumption* (New York: Zone Books, 1991), 9.

11 Natasha Singer, "For Top Medical Students, Appearance Offers an Attractive Field," *New York Times*, March 19, 2008, A1, A12.

12 Georges Bataille, "The Language of Flowers," in *Visions of Excess*, 12.

13 James George Frazer, *The Illustrated Golden Bough*, ed. Mary Douglas, illus. Sabine MacCormack (New York: Doubleday, 1978), 129.

El Mexicano

1 Sigmund Freud, *The Origins of Psychoanalysis: Letters to Wilhelm Fliess* (New York: Basic Books, 1954), 240. The word *filth* here has been glossed by Norman O. Brown as "excrement." See Brown, *Life against Death* (Middletown, CT: Wesleyan University Press, 1959), 259.

2 Alfredo Molano, *Trochas y fusiles: Historias de combatientes* (Bogotá: Punto de Lectores, 2007), 189–90.

A Rare and Beautiful Bird in Flight

1 Charles Baudelaire, "The Painter of Modern Life," in *The Painter of Modern Life and Other Essays*, trans. and ed. Jonathan Mayne (New York: Phaidon, 1964), 3.

2 David Harvey, *A Brief History of Neoliberalism* (Oxford: Oford University Press, 2005).

3 Christine Haughney, "Even in Tough Times, It Seems, a Person Needs Mascara," *New York Times*, February 28, 2009, A2.

4 Michael Ciepley and Brooks Barnes, "Americans Flock to the Movies, Seeking a Silver Lining," *New York Times*, March 1, 2009, A1.

5 Ravi Somaiya, "It's the Economy, Girlfriend," *New York Times*, January 28, 2009, A21.

6 Michael Wilson, "Looking for Security in a Cube of Steel: Sales of Home Safes Booming in a Faltering Economy," *New York Times*, March 7, 2009, A15.

7 Susan Dominus, "Not the Rolls, My Good Man: These Times Demand the Station Wagon," *New York Times*, March 2, 2009, A17.

8 Ibid.

Winnypoo

1 George R. Stewart, *Storm* (1941; Berkeley, CA: Heyday Press, 2003).

Spending

1 Henry Mayhew, *London Labour and the London Poor*, 4 vols. (1861–1862; New York: Dover, 1968), 1:2.

2 Norman Lindsay, *The Magic Pudding: Being the Adventures of Bunyip Bluegum and His Friends Bill Barnacle and Sam Sawnoff* (1918; New York: New York Review of Books, 2004).

3 Marshall Sahlins, "The Original Affluent Society," in *Stone Age Economics* (Chicago: Aldine-Atherton, 1972).

4 Nietzsche, *Twilight of the Idols* (New York: Penguin, 1990), 86.

Cool

1 L Report, "Overview," http://www.lreport.com (accessed October 9, 2008).
   Malcolm Gladwell, "The Coolhunt," *New Yorker,* March 17, 1997.
2 Walter Benjamin, "The Paris of the Second Empire in Baudelaire," in
   Charles Baudelaire: A Lyric Poet in the Era of High Capitalism, trans. Harry
   Zohn (London: New Left Books, 1973), 79.
3 Walter Benjamin, Convolut B, "Fashion," in *The Arcades Project* (Cambridge,
   MA: Harvard University Press, 1999), 62–81.
4 Fredric Jameson, "The Cultural Logic of Late Capital," *New Left Review* 146
   July/August 1984).

The Designer Smile

1 John Berger, "Drawn to That Moment," in *Berger on Drawing,* ed. Jim Savage
   (Aghabullogue, Ireland: Occasional Press, 2005), 67–72. First appeared in
   New Society, 1976; also published in the collection *The White Bird* (Hogarth
   Press, 1985).
2 Walter Benjamin, "The Storyteller: Reflections on the Works of Nicolai Leskov," in *Illuminations,* ed. Hannah Arendt (New York: Schocken,
   1968), 94.

The Designer Body

1 Daniella Gandolfo, *The City at Its Limits* (Chicago: University of Chicago
   Press, 2009), 53.
2 Roger Caillois, "Mimicry and Legendary Psychesthenia," trans. John Shepley, *October,* no. 31 (Winter 1984), 30.

Mythological Warfare

1 J. M. Coetzee, "The Vietnam Project," in *Dusklands* (London: Secker and
   Warburg, 1974).
2 William S. Burroughs, *Cities of the Red Night* (New York: Henry Holt,
   1981), 26.
3 Francois Rabelais, *The Histories of Gargantua and Pantagruel* (London: Penguin, 1955), 305–10.
4 Miguel Caballero website, http://miguelcaballero.com (accessed May 25,
   2011).
5 *New York Times,* November 18, 2011.
6 Thanks to Canadian artist and Toronto resident Mark Closier for these Internet links.
7 Walter Benjamin, "The Storyteller: Reflections on the Works of Nicolai Leskov," in *Illuminations,* ed. Hannah Arendt (New York: Schocken,
   1968), 84.

Beauty and Mutilation

1 German Guzmán Campos, Orlando Fals Borda, and Eduardo Umaña Luna, *La Violencia en Colombia*, 2 vols. (Bogotá: Ediciones Tercer Mundo, 1962 [vol. 1], 1964 [vol. 2]). Robin Kirk, *More Terrible Than Death: Massacres, Drugs, and America's War in Colombia* (New York: Public Affairs, 2003). Michael Taussig, "The Language of Flowers," in *Walter Benjamin's Grave* (Chicago: University of Chicago Press, 2006). María Victoria Uribe, *Matar, rematar y contramatar: Las massacres de la violencia en el Tolima, 1948–1964* (Bogotá: CINEP, 1990). Also, see Arnold Berleant, "Art, Terrorism and the Negative Sublime," *Contemporary Aesthetics* 7 (November 2009).

2 Andres Fernando Suarez, "Le sevicia en las massacres de la guerra colombiana," *Analisis Politica*, no. 63 (2008), 72. Cited in *La masacre de El Salado*, Grupo de Memoria Historico (Bogotá: Tauris, 2008), 82.

3 Alfredo Molano, *Ahí, les dejo esos fierros* (Bogotá: Áncora, 2009), 27.

4 Friedrich Nietzsche, *On the Genealogy of Morality* (Cambridge: Cambridge University Press, 1994), 41, 45–46.

5 Ibid., 59

The Exploding Breast

1 Karl Penhaul, "Luxuries dazzled gangster's girlfriend," CNN, October 15, 2009, http://edition.cnn.com/2009/WORLD/americas/10/15/colombia .girlfriends.

2 Walter Benjamin, *The Origin of German Tragic Drama*, trans. John Osborne (1963; London: New Left Books, 1977), 188.

Virtual U

1 Charles Baudelaire, "The Painter of Modern Life," in *The Painter of Modern Life and Other Essays* (New York: Da Capo, 1986), 12.

2 Friedrich Engels, *The Condition of the Working Class in England*, trans. and ed. W. O. Henderson and W. H. Chaloner (1845; Stanford, CA: Stanford University Press, 1968), 30–31.

3 Cited in Benjamin, *Arcades Project*, 449–50.

The History of Beauty

1 Charles Baudelaire, "The Painter of Modern Life," in *The Painter of Modern Life and Other Essays* (New York: Da Capo, 1986), 12.

2 Jean-Francois Lyotard, "Adrift," in *Driftworks* (Brooklyn, NY: Semiotexte, 1984), 14–15.

3 Ibid., 14.

4 Baudelaire, "Painter of Modern Life," 2.

5 Walter Benjamin, *The Arcades Project* (Cambridge, MA: Harvard University Press, 1999), 64.

6 Ibid.

7 D. H. Lawrence, "Nottingham and the Mining Country," in *D. H. Lawrence: Selected Essays* (London: Penguin, 1954), 120-21.

8 D. H. Lawrence, *Apocalypse* (1931; London: Penguin, 1995), 64.

9 Benjamin, *Arcades Project*, 64.

10 Bataille, *The Accursed Share: An Essay on General Economy*, vol. 2, trans. Robert Hurley (1976; New York: Zone Books, 1991), 209.

11 Guy Trebay, "Taming the Runway," *New York Times*, October 8, 2009, E6.

History of the Shoe

1 B. Traven, *The Bridge in the Jungle* (1938; New York: Hill and Wang, 1967), 21.

2 Friedrich Nietzsche, *On the Genealogy of Morality* (Cambridge: Cambridge University Press, 1994), 61.

3 Sigmund Freud, *The Origins of Psychoanalysis: Letters to Wilhelm Fliess* (New York: Basic Books, 1954).

4 Nietzsche, *On the Genealogy of Morality*, 70, 71.

5 A. Scherz, E. R. Scherz, G. Tappopi, A. Otto, *Hair-Styles, Head-Dresses and Ornaments in Namibia and Southern Afrca* (Windhoek, Namibia: Gamsberg, Macmillan, 1981), 53 (photograph by K. Schettler, number 32).

Surgeons of the Underworld

1 Roger Caillois, "The Sociology of the Executioner," in *The College of Sociology*, ed. Denis Hollier, trans. Betsy Wing, 234-47 (Minneapolis: University of Minnesota Press, 1988).

2 Ibid., 240.

3 Ibid., 243

4 Jean Genet, *The Thief's Journal* (New York: Grove, 1964), 65.

5 *El Tiempo*, August 8, 2007, 3.

6 *El Tiempo*, September 19, 2009.

The Designer Name

1 Article by Maria del Rosario Arrázola, *El Espectador*, August 14, 2008.

2 Ibid.

3 *Independent*, April 17, 2009.

4 Constanza Vieira, "Paramilitaries Don't Want to Take the Blame Alone," Inter Press Service, July 12, 2010, http://www.ipsnews.net/news.asp ?idnews=52115.

5 Alfredo Molano, *Ahí, les dejo esos fierros* (Bogotá: Áncora, 2009), 66.

6 Alfredo Molano, *Trochas y fusiles: Historias de combatientes* (Bogotá: Punto de Lectores, 2007), 123.

Law in a Lawless Land

1 Walter Benjamin, Convolut B, "Fashion," in *The Arcades Project* (Cambridge, MA: Harvard University Press, 1999), 63.
2 Giacomo Leopardi, "Dialogue between Fashion and Death," in *Essays and Dialogues* (1824; Berkeley: University of California Press, 1982), 69.
3 Gustave Flaubert, *Sentimental Education* (London: Penguin, 1964), 164.
4 Ioan P. Couliano, *Eros and Magic in the Renaissance* (Chicago: University of Chicago Press, 1987), 210.
5 Hakim Bey (Peter Lamborn Wilson), *T.A.Z.: The Temporary Autonomous Zone, Ontological Anarch, Poetic Terrorism* (Brooklyn: Autonomedia, 1985).
6 Eric J. Hobsbawm, *Interesting Times: A Twentieth Century Life* (New York: New Press, 2002), 414–15.
7 Zygmut Bauman, "Postmodern Adventures of Life and Death," in *Modernity, Medicine and Health: Medical Sociology towards 2000*, ed. Graham Scambler and Paul Higgs (London: Routledge, 1998), 226. Thanks to Ayesha Adamo for this valuable reference.
8 Michael Taussig, *Shamanism, Colonialsim, and the Wild Man: A Study in Terror and Healing* (Chicago: University of Chicago Press, 1987).
9 "Dionysus," in *The Classical Oxford Dictionary*, 3rd ed., ed. Simon Hornblower and Antony Spawforth (Oxford: Oxford University Press, 2003), 479.

The Tabooed Cleft

1 " 'Berlusconi's Fat' Moulded to Art," BBC News, June 20, 2005, http://news.bbc.co.uk/2/hi/entertainment/4110402.stm.
2 W. E. H. Stanner, "Durmurgam, A Nagiomeri," in *In the Company of Man: Twenty Portraits by Anthropologists*, ed. Joseph B. Casagrande (New York: Harper, 1960), 81, 82.
3 Roger Caillois, "Paris, mythe moderne," *Nouvelle Revue francaise* 25, no. 284 (May 1, 1937): 692, cited in Walter Benjamin, *The Arcades Project* (Cambridge, MA: Harvard University Press, 1999), 78–79.
4 Louis Aragon, *Paris Peasant* (1926; London: Jonathan Cape, 1971), 28.
5 Max Guckman, *Custom and Conflict in Africa* (Oxford: Blackwell, 1955), 110–11.
6 Walter Benjamin, Convolut B, "Fashion," in *The Arcades Project* (Cambridge, MA: Harvard University Press, 1999), 63.
7 Benjamin, *Arcades Project*, 69–70.

works consulted

Aragon, Louis. *Paris Peasant.* 1926; London: Jonathan Cape, 1971.

Arrazola, Maria del Rosario. Article in *El Espectador.* August 14, 2008.

Bataille, Georges. *The Accursed Share: An Essay on General Economy.* Trans. Robert Hurley. New York: Zone Books, 2007.

———. "Transgression." In *Erotism: Death and Sensuality.* 1962; San Francisco: City Lights,1986.

———. *Visions of Excess: Selected Writings, 1927-1939.* Trans. and ed. Alan Stoekl. Minneapolis: University of Minnesota Press, 1985.

Baudelaire, Charles "The Painter of Modern Life." In *The Painter of Modern Life and Other Essays.* Trans. and ed. Jonathan Mayne. New York: Phaidon Press, 1964.

Bauman, Zygmunt. "Postmodern Adventures of Life and Death." In *Modernity, Medicine, and Health: Medical Sociology towards 2000,* ed. Graham Scambler and Paul Higgs, 216-31. London: Routledge, 1998.

BBC News. "'Berlusconi's Fat' Moulded to Art." October 15, 2009. http://news.bbc.co.uk/2/hi/entertainment/4110402.stm.

Benjamin, Walter. *The Arcades Project.* Cambridge, MA: Belknap Press, 1999.

Benjamin, Walter. *The Origin of German Tragic Drama.* Trans. John Osborne. 1963; London: New Left Books, 1977.

———. "Theses on the Philosophy of History." In *Illuminations,* ed. Hannah Arendt. New York: Schocken, 1968.

———. "The Paris of the Second Empire in Baudelaire." In *Charles Baudelaire: A Lyric Poet in the Era of High Capitalism.* Trans. Harry Zohn. London: New Left Books, 1973.

————. "The Storyteller: Reflections on the Works of Nicolai Leskov." In *Illuminations*, ed. Hannah Arendt. New York: Schocken, 1968.

Berger, John. "Drawn to That Moment." In *Berger on Drawing*. Ed. Jim Savage. Aghabullogue, Ireland: Occasional Press, 2005.

Berleant, Arnold. "Art, Terrorism and the Negative Sublime." *Contemporary Aesthetics* 7 (November 2009).

Bey, Hakim (Peter Lamborn Wilson). *T.A.Z.: The Temporary Autonomous Zone, Ontological Anarchy, Poetic Terrorism*. Brooklyn: Autonomedia, 1985.

Brown, Norman O. "Dionysus in 1990." In *Apocalypse and/or Metamorphosis*, 158-200. Berkeley: University of California Press, 1991.

Burroughs, William S. *Cities of the Red Night*. New York: Henry Holt, 1981.

Caillois, Roger. "Mimicry and Legendary Psychesthenia." Trans. John Shepley. *October*, no. 31 (Winter 1984), 17-32.

————. "Paris, mythe moderne." *Nouvelle Revue francaise* 25, no. 284 (May 1, 1937).

————. "The Sociology of the Executioner." In *The College of Sociology*. Ed. Denis Hollier. Trans. Betsy Wing. Minneapolis: University of Minnesota Press, 1988.

Ciepley, Michael, and Brooks Barnes. "Americans Flock to the Movies, Seeking a Silver Lining." *New York Times*, March 1, 2009, A1.

Clendinnen, Inga. "The Cost of Courage in Aztec Society." *Past and Present*, no. 107 (May 1985), 16-89.

"Dionysus." In *Classical Oxford Dictionary*, 3rd ed., ed. Simon Hornblower and Anthony Spawforth. Oxford: Oxford University Press, 2003.

Dominus, Susan. "Not the Rolls, My Good Man: These Times Demand the Station Wagon." *New York Times*, March 2, 2009, A17.

Engels, Friedrich. *The Condition of the Working Class in England*. Trans. and ed. W. O. Henderson and W. H. Chaloner. 1845; Stanford, CA: Stanford University Press, 1968.

Evans-Pritchard, E. E. *Nuer Religion*. Oxford: Oxford University Press, 1956.

————. *Witchcraft, Oracles, and Magic among the Azande*. Oxford: Clarendon Press, 1937.

Flaubert, Gustave. *Sentimental Education*. London: Penguin, 1964.

Foucault, Michel. "Preface to Transgression." In *Language, Counter-Memory, Practice*, 29–52. Ithaca, NY: Cornell University Press, 1977.

Frazer, James George. *The Illustrated Golden Bough*. Ed. Mary Douglas. Illus. Sabine MacCormack. Garden City, NY: Doubleday, 1978.

Freud, Sigmund. *The Origins of Psychoanalysis: Letters to Wilhelm Fliess*. New York: Basic Books, 1954.

Gandolfo, Daniella. *The City at Its Limits*. Chicago: University of Chicago Press, 2009.

Genet, Jean. *The Thief's Journal*. New York: Grove Press, 1964.

Gladwell, Malcolm. "The Coolhunt." *New Yorker*, March 17, 1997, 78.

Harvey, David. *A Brief History of Neoliberalism*. Oxford: Oxford University Press, 2005.

Haughney, Christine. "Even in Tough Times, It Seems, a Person Needs Mascara." *New York Times*, February 28, 2009, A2.

Hobsbawm, Eric. *Interesting Times: A Twentieth Century Life*. New York: New Press, 2002.

Hubert, Henri, and Marcel Mauss. *Sacrifice: Its Nature and Function*. 1898; Chicago: University of Chicago Press, 1964.

Jameson, Fredric. "The Cultural Logic of Late Capital." *New Left Review* 146 (July/August 1984).

———. *Postmodernism, or, The Cultural Logic of Late Capitalism*. Durham, NC: Duke University Press, 1991.

Kirk, Robin. *More Terrible Than Death: Massacres, Drugs, and America's War in Colombia*. New York: Public Affairs, 2003.

Krugman, Paul. "Revenge of the Glut." Op-ed. *New York Times*, March 2, 2009, A23.

Lawrence, D. H. *Apocalypse*. 1931; London: Penguin, 1995.

———. "Nottingham and the Mining Country." In *D. H. Lawrence: Selected Essays*, 114–25. Harmondsworth: Penguin, 1954.

Leopardi, Giacomo. "Dialogue between Fashion and Death." In *Essays and Dialogues*. 1824; Berkeley: University of California Press, 1982.

Lindsay, Norman. *The Magic Pudding: Being the Adventures of Bunyip Bluegum and His Friends Bill Barnacle and Sam Sawnoff*. 1918; New York: New York Review of Books, 2004.

L Report. "Overview." http://www.lreport.com (accessed October 9, 2008).

Lyotard, Jean-Francois. "Adrift." In *Driftworks*. Brooklyn, NY: Semiotexte, 1984.

Malinowski, Bronislaw. *Argonauts of the Western Pacific*. 1922; Prospect Heights, IL: Waveland, 1984.

Mayhew, Henry. *London Labour and the London Poor*. 4 vols. 1861-1862; New York: Dover Publications, 1968.

Miller, Daniel. *A Theory of Shopping*. Ithaca, NY: Cornell University Press, 1998.

Molano, Alfredo. *Ahí, les dejo esos fierros*. Bogota: Áncora, 2009.

———. *Trochas y fusiles: Historias de combatientes*. Bogotá: Punto de Lectores, 2007.

Nietzsche, Friedrich. *The Gay Science*. Cambridge: Cambridge University Press, 2001.

———. *On the Genealogy of Morality*. Cambridge: Cambridge University Press, 1994.

———. *Twilight of the Idols*. New York: Oxford University Press, 1998.

Paternostro, Silvana. "Tetas y paraiso." *Gatopardo*, June 2011.

Penhaul, Karl. "Luxuries Dazzled Gangster's Girlfriend." CNN. October 15, 2009. http://edition.cnn.com/2009/WORLD/americas/10/15/colombia.girlfriends/.

Rabelais, Francois. *The Histories of Gargantua and Pantagruel*. London: Penguin, 1955.

Sahlins, Marshall. *Stone Age Economics*. Chicago: Aldine-Atherton, 1972.

Scherz, A., E. R. Scherz, G. Tappopi, and A. Otto. *Hair-styles, Headdresses and Ornaments in Southwest Africa, Namibia and Southern Angola*. Windhoek: Gamsberg Macmillan, 1981.

Sieber, Roy, Frank Herreman, and Niangi Batulukisi. *Hair in African Art and Culture*. New York: Museum for African Art, 2000.

Singer, Natasha. "For Top Medical Students, Appearance Offers an Attractive Field." *New York Times*, March 19, 2008, A1, A12.

Solnit, Rebecca. *Wanderlust: A History of Walking*. New York: Viking, 2000.

Somaiya, Ravi. "It's the Economy, Girlfriend." *New York Times*, January 28, 2009, A21.

Stanner, W. E. H. "Durmurgam, A Nagiomeri." In *In the Company of Man: Twenty Portraits by Anthropologists*, ed. Joseph Casagrande, 63-100. New York: Harper, 1960.

Stewart, George R. *Storm*. 1941; Berkeley, CA: Heyday Press, 2003.

Suarez, Andres Fernando. "Le sevicia en las massacres de la guerra colombiana." *Analisis Política* 63 (2008).

Taussig, Michael. "The Language of Flowers." In *Walter Benjamin's Grave*, 189–218. Chicago: University of Chicago Press, 2006.

———. *Law in a Lawless Land*. Chicago: University of Chicago Press, 2003.

———. *My Cocaine Museum*. Chicago: University of Chicago Press, 2004.

———. *Shamanism, Colonialism, and the Wild Man: A Study in Terror and Healing*. Chicago: University of Chicago Press, 1987.

Traven, B. *The Bridge in the Jungle*. 1938; New York: Hill and Wang, 1967.

Trebay, Guy. "Taming the Runway." *New York Times*, October 8, 2009, E6.

Turner, Victor. "Betwixt and Between: The Liminal Period in *Rites de Passage*." In *The Forest of Symbols*, 93–111. Ithaca, NY: Cornell University Press, 1967.

Uribe, María Victoria. *Matar, rematar y contramatar: Las massacres de la violencia en el Tolima, 1948–1964*. Bogota: CINEP, 1990.

Vieira, Constanza. "Paramilitaries Don't Want to Take the Blame Alone." Inter Press Service, July 12, 2010. http://www.ipsnews .net/news.asp?idnews=52115.

Wilson, Michael. "Looking for Security in a Cube of Steel: Sales of Home Safes Booming in a Faltering Economy." *New York Times*, March 7, 2009, A15.

Wissing, Egon. "Protocol of the Experiment of March 7, 1931." In Walter Benjamin, *On Hashish*. Cambridge, MA: Harvard University Press, 2006.

index

Burroughs, William S.: "beauty is doomed," x; "the black hole," 60

Caballero, Miguel (Bogotá designer of bulletproof clothes), 61
Caillois, Roger: and the executioner, 110-12; and fashion, 143; and mimesis, 58
Cambio Extremo, 48
cartago, and narcos, 71
Carter, Jon, 141
Castro, Fidel, 124
cemetery, 25; and the church, 137; and gang funerals, 137
Cesbén, Gustavo (tailor and gold miner of Santa María), 132-35
Chávez, Hugo, 124
Chupeta, 112-14, 116
Coetzee, J. M., and mythological warfare, 60
Collége de Sociologie, 110
consumerism, x, 16, 29; and Henry Mayhew's vagabonds, 3-31; as "muscular," 30
Coral Gardens and Their Magic (Malinowski), 3
Couliano, Ion, 130
Croydon boots, 102-3

dandy, 38
Dating a Banker Anonymous, 17
depense, 3, 7-8; and agribusiness, 21-22; and the cemetery, 25; and consumerism, 31; and the devil, 151-53; and drug lords, 12; "exuberance as beauty," 25; and the guerrilla, 12-14; and laughter in the homeless shelter, 26; and my own, 15; and naming, 118; and plastic bags, 21; and the recession of 2009-2011, 16-19; as story itself, 10; and Wall Street, 32. *See also* Bataille, Georges; taboo; transgression
destape (uncovering), analogy with agribusiness and landscape, 107-9; and young women's fashion, 83-84
devil: and *depense*, 153; and increasing production on plantations, 150; replaced by stories about cosmic surgery gone wrong, 151-53

Dialectical Image (Benjamin): and Benjamin's idea of, 95; and D. H. Lawrence's sewing machine, 92; and Lyotard's concept of *drift*, 97; and photograph of the young girl, 95-96; reading backwards in order to read the future, 95; and the windlass, 92-93, 94
disfigurement, ix. *See also* mutilation
domination of nature, 2
drift (concept of J. F. Lyotard), 84, 97
Duchamp, Marcel (readymades), 24
Durkheim, Emile, 145

Engels, Friedrich, 80
Evans-Pritchard, beauty and Nuer cattle, 2-4
excess, x. See *depense*

fairytales, ix, 28; and cosmic surgery, ix, 1, 109-10; and liposuction surgery, 140-41. *See also* fat
FARC, 12-13. *See also* Arenas, Jacobo; Marulanda, Manuel (leader of the FARC)
fashion: and allegory, 98; and Baudelaire, 84; and Benjamin, 38, 84; and Benjamin's "Theses on the Philosophy of History," 130; and the cadaver (Benjamin), 127; and "collective dream energy of a society"(Benjamin), 84; and cool, 38; and drill (*"el clasico"*), 128; fashion becomes fashionable, 51; and the foot, 104; and a history of beauty, 86; and legal codes and revolution, 84; in the mid-twentieth century in Puerto Tejada, 73, and surrealism, 84; and work clothes, 87; and the young today, 73
fat: and herbs to reduce fatness, 149-50; mystique of, 141-43; sign of wealth, 150. *See also* liposuction
fingerprints, 119
flaneur, 80
Flaubert, Gustave (and *Sentimental Education*), 129-30
Foucault, Michel; and the idea of the panopticon in relation to the scotoma, 79